Learning One-to-One

Cambridge Handbooks for Language Teachers

This series, now with over 40 titles, offers practical ideas, techniques and activities for the teaching of English and other languages providing inspiration for both teachers and trainers.

Recent titles in this series:

Learner Autonomy
A guide to developing learner responsibility
ÁGOTA SCHARLE and ANITA SZABÓ

Personalizing Language Learning
GRIFF GRIFFITHS and KATHRYN KEOHANE

Teaching Adult Second Language Learners
HEATHER MCKAY and ABIGAIL TOM

Teach Business English
SYLVIE DONNA

Teaching English Spelling
A practical guide
RUTH SHEMESH and SHEILA WALLER

Using Folktales
ERIC K. TAYLOR

Learner English (Second edition)
A teacher's guide to interference and other problems
EDITED BY MICHAEL SWAN and BERNARD SMITH

Planning Lessons and Courses
Designing sequences of work for the language classroom
TESSA WOODWARD

Teaching Large Multilevel Classes
NATALIE HESS

Using the Board in the Language Classroom
JEANNINE DOBBS

Writing Simple Poems
Pattern poetry for language acquisition
VICKI L. HOLMES and MARGARET R. MOULTON

Laughing Matters
Humour in the language classroom
PÉTER MEDGYES

Stories
Narrative activities in the language classroom
RUTH WAJNRYB

Using Authentic Video in the Language Classroom
JANE SHERMAN

Extensive Reading Activities for Teaching Language
EDITED BY JULIAN BAMFORD and RICHARD R. DAY

Language Activities for Teenagers
EDITED BY SETH LINDSTROMBERG

Pronunciation Practice Activities
A resource book for teaching English pronunciation
MARTIN HEWINGS

Drama Techniques (Third edition)
A resource book of communication activities for language teachers
ALAN MALEY and ALAN DUFF

Five-Minute Activities for Business English
PAUL EMMERSON and NICK HAMILTON

Games for Language Learning (Third edition)
ANDREW WRIGHT, DAVID BETTERIDGE and MICHAEL BUCKBY

Dictionary Activities
CINDY LEANEY

Dialogue Activities
Exploring spoken interaction in the language class
NICK BILBROUGH

Five-Minute Activities for Young Learners
PENNY MCKAY and JENNI GUSE

The Internet and the Language Classroom (Second edition)
A practical guide for teachers
GAVIN DUDENEY

Working with Images
A resource book for the language classroom
BEN GOLDSTEIN

Grammar Practice Activities (Second edition)
A practical guide for teachers
PENNY UR

Intercultural Language Activities
JOHN CORBETT

Learning
One-to-One

Ingrid Wisniewska

Consultant and editor: Scott Thornbury

CAMBRIDGE
UNIVERSITY PRESS

CAMBRIDGE
UNIVERSITY PRESS

University Printing House, Cambridge CB2 8BS, United Kingdom

Cambridge University Press is part of the University of Cambridge.

It furthers the University's mission by disseminating knowledge in the pursuit of education, learning and research at the highest international levels of excellence.

www.cambridge.org
Information on this title: www.cambridge.org/9780521134583

© Cambridge University Press 2010

First published 2010
Reprinted 2015

Printed in Italy by Rotolito Lombarda S.p.A.

A catalogue record for this publication is available from the British Library

Library of Congress Cataloguing in Publication data

Wisniewska, Ingrid.
   Learning one-to-one / Ingrid Wisniewska.
      p. cm. – (Cambridge handbooks for language teachers)
   Includes index.
   ISBN 978-0-521-13458-3
   1. Language and languages–Study and teaching.   I. Title. II. Series.

P51.W57 2010
418.0071–dc22

2010017359

ISBN 978-0-521-13458-3 Paperback and CD-ROM

Contents

Thanks and acknowledgements   viii

Introduction   1

Part 1: Basic principles   6
1 Getting started   6

2 Teacher roles   17

3 Needs analysis, course design and lesson planning   36

4 Selecting and adapting materials   68

5 Feedback and reflection   89

Part 2: Activities   101
6 Conversation partner   101
    6.1   Getting to know you   101
    6.2   What do we have in common?   102
    6.3   Ask me a question   104
    6.4   Wordpool bingo   105
    6.5   Childhood pictures   106
    6.6   Your family tree   108
    6.7   Express your feelings   110
    6.8   Friends and enemies   112
    6.9   How green are you?   113
    6.10   Guess what I have   115
    6.11   Holiday postcards   116
    6.12   The power of advertising   118
    6.13   Work pie   119
    6.14   Well done!   121

7   **Observer and listener**   123
    7.1   Ask the right question   123
    7.2   Grammar auction   124
    7.3   What's the word I need?   126
    7.4   Verb cards   126
    7.5   Specialist vocabulary   128
    7.6   Tell me my story   129
    7.7   Your earliest memory   130
    7.8   Describe this room   131
    7.9   Choosing categories   132
    7.10 Picture dictation   134
    7.11 Rules and regulations   135
    7.12 The grab bag   136

8   **Feedback provider**   138
    8.1   Correcting written homework   138
    8.2   Transcribing a one-minute talk   139
    8.3   Improving your résumé   141
    8.4   Conversation sampler   143
    8.5   A job interview   144
    8.6   Leaving a phone message   147
    8.7   Tricky situations   149
    8.8   Listen to the gaps   150
    8.9   Writing a business letter   152
    8.10 Communication style   155
    8.11 Email follow-up   156
    8.12 Learning from mistakes   158

9   **Mentor and guide**   160
    9.1   Independent learning checklist   160
    9.2   Vocabulary ping-pong   162
    9.3   Phrasal verbs   163
    9.4   True friends and false friends   164
    9.5   Test-taking tips and strategies   165
    9.6   Pronunciation ranking   167
    9.7   Using your skills   168
    9.8   Visiting Second Life®   169
    9.9   Designing listening comprehension questions   172
    9.10 Listen and summarize   173

9.11	Choosing a story	174
9.12	Guessing words from context	175
9.13	Timed skim-reading	176
9.14	Going on a webquest	177
9.15	Problem-solving	179

10 Learner — **180**

10.1	Your education	180
10.2	Career paths	183
10.3	Steps in a process	185
10.4	Give a guided tour	186
10.5	Cooking lesson	187
10.6	Business etiquette	187
10.7	Museum visit	188
10.8	Selling a product	189
10.9	Cultural expert	190
10.10	Writing a description	191
10.11	Preparing a PowerPoint® presentation	192
10.12	Eating out	193
10.13	Famous entrepreneurs	194
10.14	Choosing a home	195
10.15	My favourite music	196
10.16	Culture exchange board game	197

References and further reading — **200**

Websites — **202**

Index — **204**

Thanks and acknowledgements

The author would like to give her sincerest thanks to all her former students and colleagues who inspired her to write this book. She is also thankful for the expert advice she received from Scott Thornbury and her editors, Claire Cole, Jacqueline French and Brigit Viney.

This book is dedicated to my husband Greg for his encouragement and patience.

The author and publishers acknowledge the following sources of copyright material and are grateful for the permissions granted. While every effort has been made, it has not always been possible to identify the sources of all the material used, or to trace all copyright holders. If any omissions are brought to our notice, we will be happy to include the appropriate acknowledgements on reprinting.

Text

For the text on pp. 52 Box 3.11, 158–9 Activity 8.12: Adapted from *Treatment of Error in Second Language Student Writing* by Dana R. Ferris, published by The University of Michigan Press 2002; For the text on p. 57 Box 3.15: © *Council of Europe*; For the text on pp. 75 Box 4.3, 77 Box 4.4, 79 Box 4.5 and 83 Box 4.8: Reproduced from *face2face Upper Intermediate Student's Book* by Chris Redston and Gillie Cunningham, published by Cambridge University Press 2007; For the text on p. 80 Box 4.6; Reproduced from *Ventures Level 1 Student's Book* by Gretchen Bitterlin, Dennis Johnson, Donna Price, Sylvia Ramirez and K. Lynn Savage, published by Cambridge University Press 2007; For the text on p. 82 Box 4.7: Reproduced from *Basic Grammar in Use* by Raymond Murphy, published by Cambridge University Press 2002; For the text on p. 104 Box 6.2b: Adapted from *Alternatives* by Richard Baudains and Marjorie Baudains, published by Longman 1990; For the text on p. 120 Box 6.13: Adapted from *Lessons from the Learner: Student-Generated Activities for the Language Classroom* by Sheelagh Deller, published by Longman 1990; Activity 7.2 on pp. 124–5 adapted from an idea in *Grammar Games* by Mario Rinvolucri, published by Cambridge University Press 1984; Activity 7.6 on p. 129 adapted from an idea in *Success with Foreign Languages* by Earl Stevick, published by Prentice Hall 1989; Activity 8.2 on pp. 139–140 adapted from an idea in *Doing Task-Based Teaching* by Dave Willis and Jane Willis, published by Oxford University Press 2007; Activity 8.8 on pp. 150–1 adapted from an idea in *Teaching Listening Comprehension* by Penny Ur, published by Cambridge University Press 1984; Activity 9.13 on p. 176 based on an idea in an article titled 'Two Writing Activities for Extensive Reading' by Richard R. Day, published in *English Teaching Forum* 42(3) 2004.

Commissioned artwork

Servis Filmsetting Ltd.

Introduction

Learning One-to-One is for anyone involved in teaching English or another language to individual students. Teaching an individual student offers many exciting opportunities and challenges, and this book sets out to explore how to make the most of the benefits and suggest some creative ways of meeting the challenges.

What is learning one-to-one?

There are as many types of one-to-one lessons as there are different teachers and learners, so it is difficult, if not impossible, to describe a typical one-to-one lesson. The one-to-one lesson is a unique combination of the expectations and ambitions of a teacher and a student who meet for the joint purpose of facilitating the student's language learning.

One-to-one lessons can take place in a wide variety of settings – at work, at home, in a café or restaurant, a public library, a park – and at any time of day. In fact, it is the flexibility of one-to-one learning that makes it an attractive option for people who have non-routine schedules or who are unable to commit to classes at the same time each week. Distance learning via the internet makes this flexibility even more attractive – students can log on whenever they have an hour or so of free time and talk to their teacher online.

The nature of the one-to-one relationship can also vary considerably. You might teach for a language school that offers one-to-one lessons, either in the school or in the student's workplace. You may be giving private lessons in addition to your normal teaching job. You may be tutoring school students after school, or helping adult students with work or study skills.

The content of your lessons will also depend on the context and the needs of your student. Your lessons might focus on English for conversation, for business, for travel or for exams. They may concentrate mainly on language skills, or on grammar or pronunciation. Alternatively, they may be designed to help with a very specific task such as passing an interview exam, or giving a presentation.

Whatever your teaching context, working with individual students can be a very rewarding experience, offering many learning opportunities for both you and your student.

What are the advantages of one-to-one?

Why do students choose one-to-one?

- 'Learning one-to-one gives me the opportunity to learn at my own pace.'
- 'I know that I learn best by participating actively in a conversation with someone who speaks the language really well.'
- 'I was nervous about speaking in front of a class of students, and learning one-to-one gives me a chance to gain more confidence.'
- 'I'm too busy to go to classes every week. And when you miss one lesson, you can't catch up. I need to schedule lessons whenever I have free time.'

For the student, there are many perceived advantages to one-to-one learning. They are in a relaxed and usually informal environment, where they have to interact and communicate in the target language and where they can develop a friendly and positive personal relationship with the teacher. This can help to reduce anxiety about making mistakes. They can receive immediate feedback on their language performance, which can be very motivating. Not only do they have the undivided attention of the teacher, they can also select the materials and topics they are interested in, studying at their own level and pace. They can also learn to direct their own learning path and become more skilled at independent learning strategies.

For the teacher, there are also numerous advantages to one-to-one. There is a more natural flow of communication as you engage in authentic conversation or carry out real-life tasks together. The friendly and informal relationship can be less demanding than managing a group of students in a classroom. You can get to know your student better and build up a clearer profile of their language needs. As you learn more about your student, you can weave more of their personal information into language practice activities to make them more meaningful. You can closely monitor your student's responses during the lesson, which will help you fine-tune your lessons to their language level. Lessons can be more collaborative as you choose topics and materials together, and there are many opportunities to learn from your student's knowledge and experience.

Box Introduction 1: Summary of advantages

(Please add more of your own.)

Advantages for the student	Advantages for the teacher
There is a relaxed and informal learning environment, which may be less stressful than learning in a group.	There is a more natural flow of communication.
You can develop a positive personal relationship with your teacher.	You can get to know your student better and understand their language needs.
You can get immediate feedback from your teacher.	You can monitor your student's understanding more closely.
You can select materials and topics that are relevant to you.	You can personalize your language materials to make them more meaningful for your student.
You can study at your own level and pace.	You can tailor your lessons to the language level of your student.
You can direct your own learning path and become more independent.	You can collaborate with your student on designing lessons and choosing materials.

From *Learning One-to-One* © Cambridge University Press 2010   PHOTOCOPIABLE

What are the challenges of one-to-one?

What problems do students have with one-to-one?

- 'My teacher corrects every sentence I say and it makes me nervous.'
- 'I don't always understand the grammar explanations.'
- 'I'm not good at speaking . . .'
- 'My teacher always asks me to think of next week's topic, but I think she can decide, I don't mind what we study.'

The challenges of learning one-to-one for the student are the mirror image of its advantages. Despite the friendly and informal atmosphere, the student is constantly required to participate, which can be stressful for some students. There is no opportunity to follow along by seeing what others are doing or to compare progress with other students, which can result in loss of motivation. There is also less variety in the interaction. Some students might feel more self-conscious about making mistakes as their errors may seem to be under the spotlight. Although they are getting more attention from the teacher, overemphasis on correcting errors can be discouraging. In addition, students who choose one-to-one lessons often do so because of busy schedules and work commitments. This means that lessons can sometimes occur at irregular intervals of time and this can make it difficult to feel a sense of progress.

For the teacher, the challenges are also significant. As mentioned above, interacting one-to-one with the same person for an hour or more can be very tiring. You cannot take advantage of group or pair work to stop talking for a while and reflect on how to proceed next. Materials may seem to get covered more quickly as a result. It can be difficult to provide variety in the lessons. In a classroom, you might alternate speaking activities with reading or writing, but feel more reluctant to do so in a one-to-one setting. Differences between teacher and student expectations can also become magnified. There may be a tendency to feel you have to converse all the time, for example, or that you are expected to correct all of your student's errors.

From a practical point of view, it can be a problem when lessons are cancelled by the student at the last minute. It can also be difficult, if you are travelling from place to place, to take all the materials that you might have to hand in a classroom setting. Finally, one-to-one teachers often work alone and may therefore not have the opportunity to seek advice from, or share experiences with, their colleagues.

The organization of this book

The book is divided into two parts: the first gives an overview of the areas of methodology that are most relevant to one-to-one teaching, and the second consists of activities for you to use in your lessons. A symbol ⊚ appears alongside all photocopiable materials that are available as PDFs on the CD-ROM accompanying this book.

Part 1 has five chapters. *Chapter 1* discusses the choices available with regard to teaching tools, the physical location and set-up, and the use of non-verbal communication. *Chapter 2* outlines the roles you can emphasize in your interaction with the learner. In *Chapter 3*, there are some suggestions for designing your course and planning your lessons. *Chapter 4* offers some ideas for selecting and adapting published materials. *Chapter 5* suggests some ways to facilitate your own professional development.

Box Introduction 2: Summary of challenges

(Please add more of your own.)

Challenges for the student	Challenges for the teacher
You have to participate constantly, which can be tiring and stressful.	There is no 'down' time to plan the next step of your lesson.
You cannot compare your progress with other students.	Materials can seem to get covered more quickly.
There is less variety of interaction.	It is more difficult to provide variety and can be difficult to maintain motivation.
You may feel more self-conscious about making mistakes.	You can feel pressured to teach according to your student's expectations.
Your expectations of the lesson may be very different from your teacher's.	Differences in expectations can become magnified.
Lessons can be at irregular intervals due to outside demands.	Lessons can be cancelled at short notice.
	You do not always have access to the materials you need.
	You do not always have the opportunity to talk with colleagues.

From *Learning One-to-One* © Cambridge University Press 2010   PHOTOCOPIABLE

Part 2 also has five chapters. These are organized according to the five teacher roles described in *Chapter 2*: conversation partner, observer and listener, feedback provider, mentor and guide, and learner. Each chapter contains activities that illustrate how you can choose to emphasize each respective role and how that role can be integrated into your lessons so that they are enjoyable and rewarding for you and your student.

PART I Basic principles

1 Getting started

Reflection
Think back to your last experience of teaching one-to-one. Visualize the setting: the room, the furniture, the window, the light, the background, the chair you were sitting in, any background noises. How were you sitting? In a relaxed or a formal way, facing your student or sitting at an angle? Take a moment to close your eyes and visualize the scene. Keep it in your mind's eye as you read the following sections.

Before starting to think about the content of your lessons, it is a good idea to consider some very general aspects of one-to-one teaching. These general aspects include an awareness of the location and physical set-up of your study area, what kinds of teaching tools to select, the importance of establishing some basic ground rules and how to use non-verbal communication to maximum benefit. This chapter looks at each of these general aspects and their potential impact on your lessons, and suggests some ways to help you facilitate a positive learning atmosphere in your lessons.

Setting up a study area

If you are teaching in your own home, you can set up a study area that is a welcoming and pleasant learning environment. You may consider introducing materials and displays to create an engaging backdrop to learning. Posters, a simple noticeboard with frequently changing items, such as postcards, newspaper articles, photos and other realia, on the wall can all help to create an atmosphere that stimulates, motivates and supports the learning of English.

Setting up your teaching tools, e.g. laptop and audio player, before the lesson starts is a sign of professionalism and shows that you are serious about starting the lesson on time. It is also important to think about lighting and background noise. You might have to strike a compromise between sitting near a sunny window or competing with a lot of outside noise. The background ambience of the room can really affect the comfort and motivation of both you and your student, so it is a good idea to notice whether a room is too hot, stuffy, noisy or bright and think of solutions to this early on.

Home study area

Office study area

Learning One-to-One

Think about how to arrange the chairs and table for your lesson. Sometimes your choices are limited because you are teaching in a classroom, or in a company office or meeting room. However, a variety of seating arrangements is usually possible (see illustrations below), depending on your preferred teaching style and what is most appropriate for your lesson.

Facing across the table

At an angle of the table

Sitting facing your student in interview style will make the lesson more formal, while sitting at adjacent sides of the table corner can be more convenient for looking at a laptop or a book together. Experimenting with seating arrangements and rearranging chairs and tables can help to increase motivation and make certain activities run more efficiently.

Side by side

Away from the table

Teaching tools

If you are teaching in a company or office setting, you may not have access to all the teaching aids of the classroom. It might be possible to ask the company to provide some basics such as a small whiteboard with markers, an audio player and a good dictionary. If this is not possible, then probably the most useful tool you can buy will be a small portable recording and audio-playing device. This will give you the opportunity to introduce other sources of listening input (which will also take the focus off you and give you a break) and enable you to record your student's voice with the potential for all kinds of extra grammar or fluency work.

It is also a good idea to start a collection of interesting pictures from magazines that you can use as starting points for different topics (one advantage of one-to-one is that you can examine individual pictures in detail, which generates a lot of language). Other portable materials that you might consider are: lined and blank paper for drawing, coloured pens and a set of cuisenaire rods (small coloured wooden blocks) for a more visual and kinesthetic approach.

Technology option

If you have a laptop, you can assemble useful links on your desktop or on a smartboard for easy access. These might include links to video and audio clips, news articles and other authentic material, You can put shortcuts to various online tools on your desktop, for example an online dictionary, a searchable corpus, a grammar reference website, Wikipedia®, mutual editing tools (such as Google Docs™ and Twiddla), a collection of pictures in an online picture library (such as Flickr®), a link to real worlds (such as Google Earth™) or virtual worlds (such as Second Life®) and links to some English language games websites. Not only can you use these as reference tools during your lessons, but if you have a spare five minutes at the end of a lesson, you can also introduce your student to these and other sites that will help them in their independent learning.

Discussing some ground rules

Misunderstandings about the basic ground rules concerning issues such as payments, lateness and absences can seriously affect the atmosphere of your one-to-one lessons. If you are teaching for a language school or private company, these rules may already be laid out, but if you are teaching privately, it is important to clarify them in order to avoid confusion and disagreement later. Cultural differences about lateness or absences can also cause misunderstandings. What happens if your student is late? Do you extend the lesson time and possibly run late for your next lesson? If your student does not turn up, will you still get paid? Some teachers like to use a kind of written agreement that sets out the basic rules. Others prefer to negotiate this more informally. Either way, it is an important part of the relationship between teacher and student, and a successful negotiation of the ground rules ahead of time will help things run more smoothly. The example in *Box 1.1* can be adapted to your own context.

> ## Box 1.1: Rules of our teaching/learning agreement
>
> Our lessons will be once / twice / .... times a week.
> Our lessons will be for one hour / 90 minutes / ....
> I will do 30 minutes of homework before each lesson.
> If I am more than 20 minutes late, the lesson will be cancelled.
> If I am more than 10 minutes late, the lesson will finish at the agreed time.
> If I want to cancel the lesson, I will tell you by phone or email 24 hours in advance (or fee will be paid in full).
>
> Signed .... Date ....
>
> From *Learning One-to-One* © Cambridge University Press 2010   PHOTOCOPIABLE

Technology option

If you are tutoring by email (and if you communicate with your student by email outside your lessons), you may want to share some basic guidelines about email etiquette with your student at the start of your course. (See *Box 1.2* on p. 12 for examples of the kinds of features you could discuss.) It is always a good idea to spellcheck your email messages, even short informal ones. You can also enter your student's name into your customized spellchecker to avoid errors.

Box 1.2: Email etiquette

From: Maria

> **Use a clear title for your message.**
> Examples:
> English lesson on Monday
> English homework
> English grammar query

To: Julie

Subject: Our next English lesson

> **Use polite greetings.**
> Examples:
> (formal)
> Dear Mr Williams
> (informal)
> Hello Michelle
> Hi Victor

Dear Julie,

> **Use spaces between parts of your email.**

> **Start your email with a friendly question.**
> Examples:
> How's the weather over there today?
> Did you have a good weekend?

How are you today? I'm sorry but I would like to change the time of our next lesson because I have a dentist's appointment. Could we please meet at 5 pm instead of 3 pm?

Thank you for your lesson last week. It was fun!

> **Finish your email with a friendly comment.**
> Examples:
> Thank you for your help.
> Talk to you soon.
> I hope all is well with you.
> Have a good weekend.

> **Check your spelling and punctuation.** Use exclamation marks sparingly (one per email is usually enough).
> **Use capital letters only when needed.** Using all capitals has the effect of shouting and may seem impolite. Chunks of text written in capitals can also be difficult to read.

Best wishes,

> **Use polite closings.**
> Examples:
> (formal)
> Kind regards
> (informal)
> All the best
> See you soon

Maria

Non-verbal communication

Your non-verbal communication can convey a great deal about your relationship with your student. As mentioned above, the way you arrange the chairs and table can be formal or less formal. Similarly, the way you sit can have degrees of formality. Visualize yourself in your last lesson. Are your legs or arms crossed? Are you sitting facing your student or at an angle? Are you looking at your student and smiling, or looking at the ceiling or the floor or at your notes? These questions are intended to start you thinking about the way you naturally use your body language to communicate in the one-to-one setting.

As many of these gestures are often used unconsciously, it is helpful to focus on them to think about what they are telling you and how to use them effectively. Studies of body language show, for example, that crossed arms can signal defensiveness or hostility, and by doing this you may unintentionally be signalling to your student that you are anxious or apprehensive.

While you are observing your own body language, also notice how your student is responding. For example, when you sit back in a relaxed fashion, does your student do the same, or are they still in a formal seated position at the desk? One reason might be that they do not consider this a real part of the lesson and are waiting for you to get started (see the section on signalling phases of the lesson, below). Another reason may be cultural. The student shows their respect for your authority by maintaining respectful body language. In some cultures, the relationship between a female teacher and a male student (or vice versa) may necessarily have to be a more formal one for your student to feel comfortable.

Degrees of formality can also be expressed by the type of clothing we choose to wear. In business English contexts, for example, it may be more appropriate to wear a suit, but formal clothing can also help to establish authority when required. Casual clothing may be in tune with your ideal teacher–student relationship of informal learning but might also give the impression that you do not take the lessons too seriously. Schools and companies often have a dress code for this reason.

What other non-verbal signals do you have at your disposal? Visualize your lesson again. What do you usually do while your student is talking? Are you nodding and making eye contact? Are you smiling? These are all signals of active and interested listening and will encourage your student to talk. However, you may sometimes want to play the role of evaluator while your student is talking, making notes for later error correction or discussion.

In this case you might turn slightly away from your student, looking down at your notebook and making notes, perhaps nodding from time to time as encouragement. It is difficult to be an active conversation partner and evaluator at the same time, so this will help to differentiate the roles and enable you to take more effective notes. If you use this technique, it's a good idea to explain what you are going to do and why beforehand.

Using non-verbal communication to signal phases of a lesson

When teaching a group of students, you can signal phases of the lesson using non-verbal means, for example speaking more loudly while pointing to the board to show that you are providing evaluative feedback. At another point in the lesson, you may use a softer tone of voice and different body language to signal a more informal tone when exchanging opinions with students. When teaching one-to-one, a different set of resources is available to you for this type of role-switching.

Let us suppose that you start your lesson in a relaxed and informal manner, as a conversation partner. You might choose to start the lesson with a relaxed talk, sitting back in your chair, perhaps with your chair pushed back from the table. The next phase of your lesson plan is a review of the grammar exercise your student did for homework. You may indicate a more formal approach by sitting up straight, straightening your chair to the table, picking up a pen, straightening your notes, and accompanying this with a verbal signal, such as 'OK. Let's do some serious grammar for a while.' This will help if your student is inclined to prefer chatting and will also have a positive effect on students who like a more formal approach.

After this you might decide to go over some written homework with your student. As you both need to look at the same page, it might make sense to move your chairs side by side so you can both look at the text at the same time. This has an additional advantage of focusing the student's eyes on the page and the corrections, instead of looking and interacting with you visually.

In the next phase of your lesson, you may want your student to take over control of the lesson by playing a recording and pressing the pause button when they want to ask you a question. How can you signal this change of role non-verbally? One way is to physically move the audio recorder or laptop over to the student's side of the table. Another way is simply to exchange seats with your student.

It is a good idea to take breaks at regular intervals, especially if your lesson is a long one. Use the break to stand up and walk around, or get a glass of water or cup of coffee. You can also change the chairs around if this is more appropriate for a different activity. Breaks are good for maintaining concentration, as well as for signalling different phases of your lesson.

Technology option

For online tutors using video conferencing tools, or VoIP (Voice over Internet Protocol, a telephone connection using the internet) modes with webcam, the physical environment, your clothing and body language can also influence the relationship with your student, as can the physical environment of your 'classroom' as shown by the camera. Many of the points mentioned above are relevant to online tutoring. You can arrange your 'classroom' or desk to look bright, cheerful, busy, calm or fun. You can wear formal or casual clothing. You can use objects around you as prompts for discussion and example.

For tutors using email, there are many features of email that can be used to compensate for the absence of face-to-face communication. These include:

- choice of font, font size and colour (These can be used to differentiate personal communication from grammar explanation.)
- use of colour highlighting, italics and underlining (These can be used to emphasize key points in an explanation.)
- use of layout (Spacing your comments or questions or presenting them as bulleted lists can make them more accessible.)
- use of emoticons (These can be used to respond to comments in your student's emails.)
- use of pictures (Some teachers add their own photo to their email signature to make their emails seem more personal.).

All of these features can be used to make your emails seem friendlier and more supportive. An additional idea is to use the signature function of your email to insert motivating phrases at the end of your message. You can add something like a proverb, a 'word of the day' or a quiz question, changing them on a weekly basis.

Cultural differences

In contexts where you do not share your student's culture, awareness of cultural differences in non-verbal communication will also help to avoid possible misunderstandings. It is good to be aware of cultural taboos in body language. In some cultures (Thailand or Egypt, for example), it is insulting to point the sole of your foot towards another person. In Arab cultures, the 'thumbs up' and the 'OK' sign are insults. There are also cultural differences in turn-taking styles. In some cultures, it is polite to wait for the other speaker to pause before taking your turn. In other cultures, speakers tend to continue talking until the other speaker interrupts. Such cultural differences (in addition to differences in personality and language proficiency) may help explain why your student seems reluctant to speak, or speaks too much.

Summary
This chapter discussed the following features of one-to-one teaching:
- arrangement of seating and furniture
- teaching tools to bring to the lesson
- ground rules for your lessons
- non-verbal communication
- cultural differences.

Conclusion

When meeting your student for the first time, you will probably be trying to focus on speaking and listening to your student, and it is easy to forget about the effect of environmental factors and non-verbal communication on your lesson. These factors can, however, play an important role in facilitating language learning. Their effects may become magnified in a one-to-one context where teacher and student have the chance to observe each other and their environment intensively. Thinking about how to set up your study area and teaching tools, as well as discussing some ground rules and reflecting on your use of non-verbal communication, can all help make your lessons run more smoothly.

2 Teacher roles

Reflection
Think back to your last experience of teaching one-to-one and
characterize your role in terms of a single noun. Did you feel that your
role was similar to that of a friend or adviser, or perhaps more that of
an authority figure?

Learning one-to-one offers a unique opportunity to develop a close relationship with your student, enabling you to fine-tune your methods and materials to the needs of the individual. Creating a friendly relationship is naturally conducive to maintaining a positive and relaxed learning environment. At times, the lesson can seem to be more of a learning conversation. At other times, you may feel it is necessary to provide more structure and take a more evaluative role in order to maintain motivation and ensure a sense of progress.

Although a teacher can have many roles, and these roles can shift and switch back and forth, it can be helpful to try to describe the nature of some of these roles and by doing so try to identify the qualities and skills that we feel we already possess and some that perhaps we would like to develop more. In the context of one-to-one teaching, it can be even harder to isolate the different roles that we choose or that are assigned to us. The constant interaction with one individual makes it difficult to step back and observe, describe and record. However, becoming aware of the different roles that we have in our relationship with a student can help to deal with some of the challenges of one-to-one teaching. Using these different roles as a framework to think about lessons can help to introduce variety, reduce the possible stress of constant interaction with one person and maintain student motivation.

In this chapter, I will identify some of the roles of a one-to-one teacher. This list is by no means exhaustive, and I hope that after reading, you will find points to agree and disagree with, as well as thinking of other roles that have not been mentioned. The roles I have chosen to describe are:

1 Conversation partner
2 Observer and listener
3 Feedback provider
4 Mentor and guide
5 Learner

In *Part 2* of this book, you will find suggestions for activities organized according to the type of teacher role you would like to emphasize.

Conversation partner

> *Reflection*
> *If you were having conversation lessons in a foreign language, how do you think your teacher could best help you improve? What things would help you and what things wouldn't help at all?*

For many teachers and students, the one-to-one relationship is the ideal learning model because it most resembles the natural mode of communication between people. It facilitates learning in a natural, relaxed, informal environment where students need not feel worried about looking foolish in front of others. This can help learners to feel less inhibited and therefore more receptive to language input. As conversation partners, we can exchange real opinions and information on topics that genuinely interest both participants, diverting excessive attention to mistakes (and therefore feelings of success or failure) to the real communicative content of the exchange.

Some students, perhaps particularly those who are at an advanced level, may feel satisfied with 'just conversation' and may use the teacher as more of a language/cultural informant. But although conversation will be an important part of any one-to-one lesson, most learners will probably not feel much sense of progress if the one-to-one lesson consists solely of conversation.

As a teacher and conversation partner, we can adjust the language level of our speech to the level of our student. This means not only making sure that our language level is comprehensible to the learner, but also raising the level slightly above that of our student to provide challenge and opportunity to learn. Vygotsky's concept of the Zone of Proximal Development (ZPD) offers a useful model for helping learners learn. The ZPD is the difference between what a learner can do without help and what they can do with the help of a teacher or a peer at a slightly higher level of competence. In language learning, this helping process is often described as 'scaffolding', in other words, providing learners with the means to learn how to do tasks by themselves. An example of scaffolding could be something like this:

Student:	I very much look to enjoy my trip to Rome next week.
Teacher:	Oh, you're looking forward to it?
Student:	Yes, I'm looking forward to it.
Teacher:	Good! I think Rome is an exciting city, isn't it?

As a conversation partner, however, the teacher is called upon not only to participate actively in an ongoing dialogue, but also to facilitate the participation of the learner, which can sometimes require more than just normal conversational skills. The one-to-one teacher can use different types of questions to 'lead' or 'follow' the learner and help them explore the learning path that suits them best. Using open questions such as 'What were language classes like when you were at school?' may open up a wide range of possible responses, giving both of you ideas for further linguistic exploration (or may lead you into unnecessarily difficult territory). Closed questions such as 'Were teachers in your school very strict?' will produce a narrower range of responses. Questions can vary on a scale from closed to open depending upon the range of responses that are possible. Look at the following exchanges. In the first exchange, the student is limited by the question types and the exchange becomes rather teacher-dominated. In the second exchange, the first (closed) question is used to lead into a topic, and open questions then help the student to explore the topic.

Teacher:	Do you travel a lot in your job?
Student:	Yes, I do. I travel a lot.
Teacher:	Do you travel every week, or every month?
Student:	Yes, once or twice a month.
Teacher:	Do you like to travel?
Student:	It's not bad.

Teacher:	Do you like your job?
Student:	Yes, I do.
Teacher:	What do you like about it?
Student:	I can travel. I go to Paris and Madrid. I like to visit different cities.
Teacher:	It sounds exciting. Which city do you like best?

It can be easy to forget that the learner is usually under a great deal more stress than you are: trying to think in a foreign language, trying to listen and understand and work out what to say, not to mention the fear of making mistakes and looking stupid. All of these thought processes take time and mental energy, and it is therefore unrealistic to expect the flow of conversation to be the same as between two native speakers. Students may not respond instantly to all our questions, and the 'conversation' may at times be somewhat stilted, with frequent pauses as we wait for a response. This wait time is, however, very important, and we should not try to hurry forward simply in order to preserve the feeling of a natural conversation. The more we jump in and try to fill the silence, the less likely it is that the learner will take the opportunity to speak. Unlike the classroom situation, where the teacher can turn to another student if the first student is not ready, the one-to-one teacher feels the burden of making every minute count by using it to talk. And this can sometimes result in the teacher talking more than is necessary.

Technology option

If you are conversing via text messaging or email, you will find other ways of encouraging your student: using emoticons, for example, to praise good or creative contributions, or a set of encouraging expressions that you can place on the automatic insert function of your email. In face-to-face conversation we give a lot of reassurance and feedback through facial expression and tone of voice, and this has to be replaced with some verbal equivalents in written email or text communications.

Teacher:	Today we're going to talk about doing things at work to help save the environment.
Student:	You mean like recycling?
Teacher:	That's right! [Good vocabulary! ☺] Do you have recycling options in your company?
Student:	Yes, we have recycling boxes.
Teacher:	That's a great idea. And do you use recycled paper?

Summary
- A natural and relaxed atmosphere is conducive to learning and there are more opportunities for real communication.
- A conversational approach alone is not usually sufficient for learning progress.
- The teacher can adjust language to the learner's level and provide scaffolding when appropriate.
- The teacher can use questions to follow or lead the student's language learning.
- Chatting by text or email requires giving some extra, positive feedback to replace non-verbal feedback.

Some language activities for enhancing your role as a conversation partner can be found in *Part 2, Chapter 6*.

Observer and listener

Reflection
Think of one student you have taught in a one-to-one context. What did you remember most clearly about their appearance or behaviour? How did you interpret this at the time?

The role of observer is one that you will probably find occurring simultaneously with one or more of your many other roles. Or you may find yourself switching back and forth between the role of observer and other roles as you use your observations to fine-tune your teaching. The role of observer also includes that of 'listener' as we 'listen' to how the learner is responding to the tasks and activities they are engaged in. A great advantage of one-to-one teaching is that you can constantly monitor how well the learner is responding to the lesson and adjust your methods or materials accordingly. To make the most of this role, you may choose to include some activities that enable you to take a back seat and focus on listening to your student rather than interacting with them.

In addition to observing your student's language level, you will also be able to notice what kinds of topics they find most interesting, what kinds of learning styles they have and what kinds of tasks they are most skilled at or familiar with. You will also be more sensitive to your student's level of motivation, which will probably vary according to the phase of the lesson, the topic or from one lesson to another. In many cases, these observations will be fleeting perceptions that you respond to without thinking, but sometimes it may be useful to record these observations in a more systematic way.

When observing your student, it is easy to jump to conclusions about what they are thinking. For example, if your student yawns frequently and looks tired, you may assume they are bored, when in fact they may have been working all night on finishing a report, and it is this, not your lesson, that is the cause of their apparent disinterest. Such misunderstandings are less likely to become magnified in a classroom context where we seldom focus on one individual for the whole lesson.

Trained observers in the field of social and educational research usually attempt to separate observation from evaluation and interpretation. This is a skill that requires experience and focused attention. Learning to take notes of your observations in a neutral non-judgemental way can help to train your observation skills. You can create opportunities for noting your observations either during or just after your lesson. To make this process more efficient, you might consider preparing a ready-made form that enables you to record your notes quickly. This will depend largely on your priorities for each individual student, but one possibility is to photocopy a page divided into sections as in *Box 2.1* below. The aim of these questions is to help you observe and describe facts that you can later reflect on and find alternative interpretations for, thus opening up your choices for altering and improving the teaching–learning interaction. The example in *Box 2.1* can be adapted for your own context. (See also *Chapter 5* for additional ways to reflect on your lessons.)

Observing learning styles

Every learner brings with them a history of successful (and unsuccessful) learning. They will be used to certain methods of learning and teaching and therefore deal with them well, but will find other methods difficult or unfamiliar. For this reason, one of the first things you may want to do is to find out about your learner's history of learning (see *Chapter 3*, p. 41). A student who is used to grammar explanations and a focus on accuracy, for example, may not understand the point of fluency-based conversational phases of a lesson. And although you may consider dictation a pointless mechanical activity, it may be one that your student feels successful at and that will motivate them if used appropriately.

The following are some questions to consider when observing how your student responds to your learning activities.

Deductive or inductive?
- Does your student expect you to explain a grammar rule first before attempting a task? Or do they tend to plunge in first and then ask questions later?
- Does your student respond well to metalanguage about how to learn? Or are they more interested in doing the activities? In the former case, this may indicate a preference for deductive teaching, i.e. rules first, then practice; in the latter case, a preference for working out the rules from the examples. Sometimes, a few well-chosen examples can be more effective than any explanation.

Box 2.1: Observer notes

Student's name .... Date ....

What questions did my student ask me today?	Which exercises/tasks was my student most/least enthusiastic about today?
Tomas asked about how to use the words 'sorry' and 'excuse me' in English.	*Today, Tomas seemed to enjoy the vocabulary quiz best. He got almost all the answers right, and he seemed pleased with himself. He didn't like practising the dialogue – his voice was flat with no intonation at all.*
Perhaps this means he would like to study more phrases and idioms in our lesson. Or perhaps he had a misunderstanding with someone which concerned this. Or maybe someone asked him about this at work and he didn't know the answer.	*He likes quizzes because he can feel a sense of progress. Maybe he doesn't like practising dialogues because they're not accuracy-based? Or was the dialogue too artificial? I should get him to role play some real dialogues from work with me.*
What did I notice about my student's behaviour today?	**Which exercises/tasks was I most/least enthusiastic about today?**
In today's lesson, Tomas was rather quiet and didn't want to say much.	*I liked the dialogue because of the contextualization. I didn't really explain why that was important, though.*
I thought he was tired. Maybe he didn't like the topic. Maybe he's feeling demotivated at lack of progress. Maybe he was just having a bad day!	*Maybe I liked it because it is less teacher-centred. I don't like giving tests all the time.*

From *Learning One-to-One* © Cambridge University Press 2010   PHOTOCOPIABLE

- Is your student already familiar with abstract grammar rules and concepts? If so, it may be worth tapping into this knowledge by teaching grammatical terms in English (noun, verb, tense, etc.) or using them in the L1 (if you share their L1). If grammar rules seem to intimidate them, then it may be best to refer to the rules only lightly, centring your teaching on sentence patterns and drills which will teach by example, not by explanation.

Accuracy or fluency?

- Does your student seem more motivated when you correct their mistakes, or when you listen for the meaning of what they are saying (and ignore mistakes)? These signs will tell you a great deal about their learning priorities. And if you consider that error correction is an essential part of your teaching, then it will be necessary to discuss and explain why you think this is going to help them.

Auditory, visual or kinesthetic?

- Does your student respond enthusiastically to listening tasks (audio tapes, music, dictations, etc.) or to visual tasks (e.g. looking at pictures or videos, or using graphic organizers) or to tasks where they touch and move things around (e.g. using cards, sticky notes, real objects)? The framework of multiple intelligences proposed by Howard Gardner suggests that we all have a number of different intelligences which can be utilized in language learning. We usually have one or two preferred intelligences, but this is not to say that we would not benefit from experimenting with others. As a teacher, you can observe which intelligences your student is not used to using and help them expand their repertoire of learning strategies.

Another way to observe learning styles is through insights offered by Neuro-Linguistic Programming. One example is to interpret your student's learning style by observing their eye movements. Looking upwards and to the right, for example, is said to indicate use of visual imagination; upwards and to the left is said to indicate imaginative recall.

Since most of us have a preferred style of learning, there is a tendency to assume that what works for us will work for others. Understanding your own learning style will help you to evaluate whether the materials and methods you choose are mainly influenced by your own preferred style. Using a variety of styles can not only help maximize your student's preferred learning style (which may be different from yours, and which may not always be their best strength), but also help develop their repertoires of learning strategies. This is a good way to introduce variety into your lessons and to avoid making possibly restrictive assumptions about how language learning takes place. *Part 2* of this book will suggest a number of ways to use different learning styles in one-to-one teaching.

Summary
- Observing learner behaviour and learning styles is an integral part of the teacher's role.
- Learning to observe and record these behaviours are trainable skills.
- Constant attention to the learner's responses can help maintain the learner's engagement and motivation, while helping the teacher to improve lesson quality.

Some language activities for enhancing your role as an observer and listener can be found in *Part 2, Chapter 7.*

Feedback provider

> *Reflection*
> *Think back to when you were a beginning language learner. What kinds of feedback from your teacher did you find most motivating and most demotivating?*

Feedback is one of the main tools we can use to encourage, motivate and support learning. There are many ways of providing feedback to the learner, whether by correcting mistakes, or giving encouraging comments and praise. When developing your strategies for providing feedback with an individual student, you might want to start by asking about their preferences (see *Activity 8.12: Learning from mistakes*). How will you provide the feedback? Is it instant or delayed? Is it written or spoken? And what kind of help does it provide? When we correct errors, for example, do we provide the target form right away? Or do we provide clues and hints to help learners find the target form by themselves? Discussing your approach to giving feedback with your learner can help to clarify any differences in expectation and avoid possible misunderstandings. To exploit this role to the full, you may choose to include some activities that focus on specific types of feedback and that signal phases of the lesson when you are going to focus on accuracy rather than fluency. The following section provides some options.

Providing feedback on speaking

When you are focusing on accuracy, there are a number of ways in which you can provide feedback. It can be discouraging to be told only about one's mistakes. You may want to be selective about which errors to correct – correcting only the grammar points you are currently working on, for example, or only those that really interfere with comprehension. Try to balance your comments on errors with some positive encouragement about getting some difficult constructions right, or remembering to use a particular tense. In addition, some response to the content of the message is also important to show that you have been listening and that you found it interesting. Here are some examples of different types of feedback.

Direct feedback

• Provide the correct form and ask your student to repeat it after you.

Student:	We went Miami last weekend.
Teacher:	We went *to* Miami last weekend.
Student:	We went to Miami last weekend. We stayed in the Flamingo Hotel.
Teacher:	Good.

Scaffolded feedback

• Repeat the mistake, or repeat the sentence up to the mistake, and ask your student to correct it.
• Use gestures or facial expressions to show that a mistake has been made. Give your student three chances to correct it, and then provide the correct form.
• Give some hints as to what type of mistake has been made, e.g. wrong tense, or add an 's'. Hints may include some different gestures. For example, for word order, you may mime swapping two words around as if they were cards in a sentence. For very common errors, you might think about using coloured cards, for example a card with the letter *s* for missing third-person 's', or a card with 'th' for pronunciation of this sound, and holding them up like a football referee whenever this mistake occurs.
• Reformulate the error as part of your response. For example:

Student:	I live Kingston.
Teacher:	Do you live in Kingston?
Student:	Yes, I live in Kingston.

There is sometimes the temptation to provide the target form too early, probably in our effort to keep the interaction flowing smoothly. An exchange something like this may occur:

Teacher: What did you do last weekend?
Student: I go swim.
Teacher: You went swimming?
Student: Yes.

In this exchange, the student has not produced the correct sentence, but it feels as though successful communication has taken place. Although this strategy may sometimes be useful in establishing confidence and rapport, if it is overused, it prevents the student from reaching their optimum language performance.

Delayed feedback

- While your student is speaking, write down all the mistakes. When they have finished, give them your written record to correct immediately or for homework.
- Record your student on audio and then listen to the recording and identify the errors together.

Technology option

When tutoring online via voice chat, you have the option of providing feedback in both spoken and written form. You can correct errors via text, perhaps using symbols or set phrases as hints to save time, while continuing the verbal conversation online. Or you can use the text chat to provide praise and encouragement, while maintaining verbal conversational responses.

The following is an example of a conversation that could be on Skype™ or another VoIP system that has both chat and text-messaging options.

Teacher: Did anything special happen at work this week?
Student: My boss told us we had to work late every night this week.
Teacher: Oh no! That's terrible. Are you going to? (Text message: excellent use of indirect speech with 'tell'. Well done. ☺)
Student: I don't want. But my co-workers will get angry if I will not stay.
Teacher: (Text message: if I will not stay? Tense?)

Student:	if I don't stay.
Teacher:	(Text message: That's right – it's a first conditional, very good!) Yes, it's important to get on with your co-workers, isn't it?
Student:	I don't know how to solve this problem.
Teacher:	Thank you for sharing that problem with me. I can understand it must be very difficult for you . . .

Another option is to save all text comments continuously as you go along, and then send a summary of the most useful ones at the end of the lesson. Or save the complete text transcript and ask your student to type the corrections for homework.

One of the risks of one-to-one teaching is that there may be too much of a spotlight on the student's errors. Unlike learning in a group context, where students can talk to each other independently without fear of correction, they may associate talking with the teacher with being corrected. It may help your student to know that there are certain phases of the lesson where you will focus on fluency, and others where you will focus on accuracy. Signalling these phases of the lesson can be done either verbally ('In this activity we are going to focus on fluency and I'm not going to correct your grammar') or non-verbally. One idea for a non-verbal signal is to use a 'traffic signal' where the student can choose red for constant error feedback (i.e. the focus is on accuracy); amber for feedback at the teacher's discretion; or green if they want no correction (i.e. the focus is on fluency). The same activity could be repeated with different 'settings'.

Signalling different phases of the lesson

Providing feedback on writing

With informal written work, such as journals, blogs or emails, you may not be too concerned about grammar errors. However, in formal written work, such as essays, business letters and reports, there is more likely to be a focus on accuracy. What kinds of options are available for providing feedback on written work?

a) *Direct*: Correct all the errors yourself and ask your student to rewrite their work.

b) *Scaffolded*: Use a system of codes to help your students find the errors, e.g. 'T' for tense, 'Sp' for spelling, etc.

c) *Negotiated*: Underline errors and go over them together. Talking through the errors can help to make the correction more memorable for your student and give you a better understanding of the underlying cause of the error, e.g. L1 transference, or overgeneralization.

As with spoken feedback, it can be discouraging to receive a page full of corrections. You may want to be selective about which errors to correct and balance corrections with positive comments. In addition, some response to the content of the writing is also important to show that you are interested in the meaning as well as the form. Here are some examples of responding to the content of the writing in an encouraging way.

- 'That was a great description of your first day at school, Jenny. I especially liked the way you described your first teacher. She sounds terrific – completely different from my first schoolteacher!'
- 'Thanks for telling me about your experience in Australia. It sounds like you had a fascinating time, and it made me want to go to Australia too one day.'

When giving feedback, you can also choose to model skills that you would like your student to emulate. Switching back and forth between 'telling' and 'showing' can be done far more easily in a one-to-one context than in a group. For example, while I am correcting a student's written work, I may point out how one type of error occurs several times throughout the passage. By doing this, I am not only pointing out errors to be corrected, but also showing how to look for repeated patterns, a skill that I would like my student to apply when they are checking their own work. You can make this explicit by asking questions that will lead your student to apply this skill to other types of errors, praising them for finding the patterns by themselves, or noticing particular editing skills they have developed by themselves. Some teachers record their verbal comments when correcting written work and give the recording (video or audio) to their students to use when they are redrafting.

One study of learners in an academic writing context suggested that although students' stated preference was for correction of grammar errors, they actually spent more time looking at tutors' comments on the content and ideas in their work (Anderson, Benson and Lynch, 2001). This study also indicated that students remembered feedback more if they themselves initiated the topic for discussion. Thus, asking your student to select which aspects to work on or asking them to identify the causes of errors are possible alternatives to telling students where the mistakes are. Here are some questions you could use to help elicit your student's participation in this process.

- Tell me about this paragraph. How could you improve it?
- What do you think is the main problem in this opening line?
- Can you think of another way to say. . .?
- How could you make this easier for the reader to understand?
- What type of problem do you think makes this unclear – grammar, vocabulary, syntax or something else?

The language of instruction can also have an effect on how feedback is given and received. If you share your student's first language, you may decide to give feedback in English in order to maximize opportunities for speaking English. Giving feedback in the student's L1, however, might enable them to participate more actively in the feedback process, especially for lower levels.

Technology option

If students can send their work to you by email, you can take advantage of the 'track changes' function on Microsoft® Word to add your comments electronically (see *Box 2.2*). This has several advantages. First, you can use different coloured fonts to differentiate types of corrections, e.g. grammar, vocabulary or style. You can also add comments or queries using the 'insert comment' function, and your student can reply to these comments electronically, thus creating an ongoing dialogue. As mentioned above, any kind of dialogue with your student about their work will make it more memorable for them and help you to understand their thought processes better. Second, electronic comments and corrections can be deleted and the student does not have to rewrite their work to achieve a final draft. Third, you can keep copies of all the versions so that you and your student can see how a piece of writing has developed and learn from the process.

Box 2.2: Correcting and commenting electronically

Describe the process of how to learn a foreign language.

Learning a foreign language can be fun and interesting. It is not easy learn a foreign language. There is a lot of processes to go through in order to accomplish a foreign language.

Comment [ITW1]: Good starting sentence! I'm happy to see your positive attitude!

In order for you to know a language better, you must to find a good teacher or tutor. Having a friend of that language can be very nice too. They can help you talk or know the language out of class. After finding out a person to teach you that language, you must work hard to understand what he or she is teaching.

Comment [ITW2]: Can you use a relative clause here, a friend who . . .

Comment [ITW3]: This is a little informal, can you rephrase?

Comment [ITW4]: What is the difference between find and find out?

General comments from teacher: *I'm glad to hear that you think language learning is fun. Your idea about finding a conversation friend is great! Can you tell me some more about the differences between learning in class and out of class?*

Another option is to help your student during the writing process by using a mutual editing tool such as Google Docs™ or Twiddla. This means that you and your student can work on writing or redrafting a document at the same time. You might also choose to work online by using a wiki to collaborate on creating webpages.

Summary
- Be selective about when to correct and what kinds of errors to correct.
- Use a variety of methods for giving feedback, according to the language level and response of your student.
- Use feedback to create opportunities for learning, helping your student to correct their own mistakes and become more independent.
- Signal fluency and accuracy phases of the lesson.
- Balance positive and negative feedback.
- Give feedback on meaning and content as well as form.

Some language activities for enhancing your role as a feedback provider can be found in *Part 2, Chapter 8.*

Mentor and guide

Reflection
Think about how your teachers in the past have encouraged you to learn. What kind of help or advice did you find most useful?

As a one-to-one teacher, you may frequently be asked to play the role of a mentor, guide, adviser, counsellor or coach. The kind of advice you are asked to give can range from questions about English grammar, study methods, books to read, jobs or scholarships to apply for, language schools to choose, to more personal issues. Thinking of ways to encourage your student and help them to feel a sense of progress and success is part of the job. To facilitate this process, you may choose to include some activities that focus on developing learning strategies as well as on the language itself.

As a mentor, you can also help your student develop independent learning skills by encouraging them to find ways to study out of class (see *Activity 9.1: Independent learning checklist*) and to develop study techniques such as using vocabulary cards (see *Activity 9.3: Phrasal verbs* and *Activity 9.4: True friends and false friends*) and keeping a vocabulary notebook. Helping them to reflect on their learning history as well as their learning strategies by using a journal or a learner log are other ways of encouraging learner autonomy (see *Chapter 5*). As students are not able to compare their progress with others, it may be helpful to get them to keep a record of their work (e.g. using audio recordings or a portfolio) so that they can check progress for themselves.

In addition to suggesting ways to improve learning strategies, you can also gather information about learning opportunities outside lessons. For example, is there an English language library, film club or conversation club in your area? Your student may be interested in knowing about language schools or scholarships in the UK or the USA. Exploring resources for online learning such as online dictionaries, grammar reference, language games websites, or joining an online language learning community or penpal exchange can be a useful way to practise language as well as to develop independent learning. Any materials that you gather with this information can be put to excellent use in your lessons.

Some one-to-one teachers sometimes find it a problem when students ask them for personal advice. It is helpful to set some limits on the kind of advice you can be expected to offer. Perhaps you have worked hard to build up a strong rapport with your student, and you do not want to let them down by refusing a request for help. Informal friendliness and concern can sometimes be misunderstood as a willingness to enter into a more personal relationship. If you are wary of getting into a situation were you might be asked for personal advice, you might try to focus on your other roles and make explicit the fact that you are a teacher, not a counsellor. Nevertheless, situations can arise where you unintentionally become involved in someone's personal problems or start to feel anxious about their expectations of you. In such cases, be ready to ask advice from other colleagues and try to come up with a range of possible solutions, for example choosing a different meeting location, meeting with two students instead of one, swapping students with another teacher, or suggesting your student find a qualified counsellor to help them.

Summary
- A mentor or guide helps the student to become independent by establishing good study habits and making the most of available learning resources.
- Try to anticipate the type of advice your student may need for their work or study.
- The line between mentor and counsellor can easily be crossed and it is important to establish boundaries.
- Seek advice from colleagues and others if you feel anxious about a student.

Some language activities for enhancing your role as a mentor and guide can be found in *Part 2, Chapter 9*.

Learner

> *Reflection*
> *Think back to your last one-to-one student and list three things that you learned from your lessons. How would you categorize them? What categories did you choose? Were they personal, professional or practical? Or perhaps you learned something about culture, history or business?*

Having the opportunity to learn about your student's area of expertise can be one of the most fascinating aspects of one-to-one teaching. Giving them the opportunity to share their knowledge with us, for example by asking them to prepare a short PowerPoint® presentation about an aspect of their job or research, will keep lessons interesting for you and also help to restore some equality in the balance of power, boosting the confidence of your student and encouraging them to realize that they have something to teach as well as to learn. As your student begins to assume some responsibility for the lesson, this will help to reduce the pressure of feeling that the success of the lesson depends entirely on you. As a result, you and your student can develop a collaborative approach to lessons that will make the most of the one-to-one learning context. With this in mind, you may choose to include some activities that encourage your student to take over part or all of a lesson and decide what topics and materials they want to use.

The reflective aspect of teaching also asks you to switch into the role of learner, asking yourself: What did I learn from my experience today? It is a good idea to allow five minutes at the end of every lesson to reflect on what happened, what worked well and what did not. This kind of reflection can help you to keep questioning the teaching/learning process and to avoid inaccurate assumptions about how your lessons are progressing. Here are a few examples of reflections by teachers.

- 'I learned always to have a plan, not to just "wing it".'
- 'I always had a "plan B" in case my materials were too hard, or just tanked.'
- 'There was too much chatting, and I tried to develop a more "teacherly attitude".'
- 'I found that I enjoyed lessons where my student decided what to talk about and study.'
- 'I learned about different attitudes to lateness and punctuality.'

Asking for feedback from your learner is an important way of developing as a teacher and improving your repertoire of teaching skills. Sometimes, it can be a simple verbal question at the end of the lesson: How would you like me to correct your mistakes? What helped you most in our lesson today? Which activity did you find most difficult today? Sometimes, it can be a short written questionnaire (see *Chapter 5, Boxes 5.1a–5.1g*).

Summary
- Find ways to enable your student to take on the role of teacher.
- Learning one-to-one is a two-way process – both teacher and student learn from each other in different ways.
- Find ways of expanding your learning by recording your observations and taking notes of data that you can use in different ways as a part of your reflection process.
- Ask your student for feedback regularly.

Some language activities for enhancing your role as a learner can be found in *Part 2, Chapter 10*.

Conclusion

In this chapter, I have given an overview of some of the different roles available to the one-to-one teacher. Because one-to-one teaching often seems like a conversation, it is easy to forget the range of other roles that a teacher may have. However, an awareness of these various teacher roles provides a useful framework that will not only help you to introduce variety into your lessons, but will also create a motivational and supportive learning environment in which you are able to plan lessons (even with minimal resources) that are appropriate to the personality and individual needs of your student. Explaining the different roles you choose for different phases of your lessons can also help your student to understand your teaching approach better and avoid misunderstandings. *Part 2* of this book offers a number of suggestions for adapting activities to emphasize different aspects of the teacher's role.

3 Needs analysis, course design and lesson planning

Reflection
Have you ever attended a language course where you felt that the
needs of the student were not taken into account? What do you think
were the reasons for this? How did it affect your language learning?

Identifying the language needs of your student and designing a course that matches up with them effectively is one of the most challenging aspects of one-to-one teaching. When teaching a group of students, the difficulty lies in trying to find a compromise among the aims of all the different people in the group. When working with an individual student, however, the problem lies more in helping the student to identify their goals, something they may not have thought about in detail and may state only in very general terms. When asked about how they want to learn, they might also have a very different understanding about what is implied by terms such as grammar (is it just talking about rules?) or listening (does it mean I won't say anything?). For these reasons, you may find it helpful to carry out needs analysis and course design / lesson planning activities at regular intervals while your student gradually becomes accustomed to your teaching style and is better able to negotiate with you about the lesson content and how they wish to learn.

In this chapter, I will suggest different ways of approaching the issues of needs analysis, course design and lesson planning, and discuss how best to take advantage of the benefits of one-to-one to develop a course that is suited to the language needs of your student.

Needs analysis

Reflection
Think back to the last language course you taught. How did you
decide what materials and syllabus to use? What did you find out
about your students that helped you plan your course?

One of the biggest advantages of learning one-to-one is the opportunity to tailor the aims, methods and materials of your course to the needs of the individual learner. It is therefore worth taking some time to identify those needs accurately and to explore different methods of obtaining information about them.

There are several areas of information that will help you plan your course. First is the learner's language level. In addition, it will be useful to have some background information about their job (or school), their learning goals and their learning style.

Language level

If you are teaching for a school or company, your student may already have completed a placement test prior to your first lesson. If not, then you might want to spend part of your first lesson on a placement test, or assign this for homework.

When teaching a group of students, it is important to assess language level in order to see whether students have been placed in the correct class, and it may not be practical to assess large numbers through speaking or writing. In one-to-one teaching, however, you can often get a more accurate all-round idea of your student's language level by interviewing them (recording the interview for later analysis and taking notes of errors), or asking them to write a short paragraph (see below).

Learner's background

There are many aspects of your learner's background that could help you to plan your course. For example, knowing about how they studied in the past, and why this was or was not successful, could help you choose your methods. Knowing why your student needs English will help you choose relevant materials.

Obtaining information about the learner's needs

Needs analysis questionnaires

A needs analysis is something that you can carry out periodically throughout your course as students' aims and expectations can evolve over time, and can change in response to your lessons. Different types of questionnaires can be used at different stages of your course.

The needs analysis questionnaires on pp. 40 to 48 include a variety of formats as different question types can often reveal different answers. They are intended to give you ideas for developing your own questionnaires – experimenting with different types of formats and questions – that will be more relevant to your own context.

When giving your student a written questionnaire, it is a good idea to explain why you need the information, how you will use the information and who will have access to it. If possible, try to provide questionnaires at the language level of your student. If your student is a beginner and you do not share their first language, consider offering the questions in both English and in first language versions.

Reflective writing

Ask your student to write a few sentences about themselves and read them aloud to you. This will enable you to see their writing speed, handwriting and spelling, and to evaluate pronunciation. A first homework task (depending on level) can be a short piece of writing about their language learning history, or about their aims for learning English. This will give you information about writing ability, grammar and also insights into learner needs and motivation. An alternative idea is to ask your student to write a letter to you explaining their reasons for learning English.

Journal

If you have asked your student to keep a journal as part of their learning, you can periodically suggest topics that will encourage them to share their feelings about learning. A journal can be written by hand in a notebook, typed on computer and sent by email, written in an online blog, or recorded in audio form. Here are some possible journal topics:

- Which activities and materials have you found most helpful for your work in our lessons so far?
- Which grammar points do you want more practice in?
- Describe one situation at work where you used English recently.
- Describe one conversation that you had in English recently. How did you feel about your English afterwards?
- Describe one way in which English has helped you recently.

Visiting your student's workplace

You can ask your student to invite you to visit them at work. (This is much easier if you are teaching in a company setting.) You could shadow them in their daily routine for a short time. You could also talk to their colleagues or boss, or ask for some samples of (non-confidential) work documents to take away. The picture you can build by actually seeing your student's workplace and listening to what goes on there is sometimes worth more than many hours of careful interviewing. All of this information will help you to plan a course that is appropriate to your student's needs. It is important to obtain your student's active and positive cooperation in any of these research activities.

Obtaining authentic documents or other data

Ask your student for examples of written or printed material in English from their work or study place. This will give you material to work on in the lessons, and also give you a better picture of what type and level of English is required. If your student is studying at school, try to get a copy of the textbook. If your student is aiming to pass an exam, get copies of past test papers. If your student works in a company, see if they can bring in any sample letters or emails, an instruction manual, forms or brochures. Use the internet to get information about typical tasks in this kind of job.

Another possibility is to ask your student to get sample recordings of presentations, lectures or conversations, although it may be difficult to obtain permission to make such recordings.

Needs analysis questionnaires

There are a number of ways in which needs analysis questionnaires can be used:

- Give the questionnaire as homework and go over the answers together in the next class.
- Ask your student to complete the questionnaire at the end of the lesson.
- Use the questionnaire to interview your student. They tell you what to write and you fill out the answers.
- Use the questionnaire as an outline for verbal interview and take notes as you talk. Record the interview. (The recording will be an interesting point of comparison for you and your student to evaluate progress.)
- Send the questionnaire by email. Then respond by email with questions (using different colour fonts or the 'track changes' tool) to create a collaborative document.
- Ask students to create their own questions to add to your questionnaire.

Box 3.1: Practical information questionnaire

Student's name .... Date ....

Address (home) ....

(work) ....

Telephone number (work) .... (home/mobile) ....

Email address ....

How often do you want to meet?
❑ Once a week
❑ Twice a week
Other ....

How long would you like to meet for?
❑ 30 minutes
❑ 1 hour
❑ 90 minutes
Other ....

What days and times are best for you?
(days) ....
(times) ....

Where do you want to meet? ....

If you need to cancel a lesson, please inform me at least 24 hours in advance. You will inform me: by email / by telephone / in person.

The teacher will bring the following materials for the lesson ....
....

The student will bring the following materials ....
....

From *Learning One-to-One* © Cambridge University Press 2010   PHOTOCOPIABLE

Box 3.2: Learner history questionnaire

Student's name .... Date ....

1 How long have you been learning English? ....

2 Which other languages can you speak or write? ....

3 Have you ever visited an English-speaking country? If yes, where? For how long?
   ....
   ....
   ....

4 What did you mostly study and practise in your past lessons? Rank from most
   (=1) to least important.
   - ❏ Conversation
   - ❏ Grammar
   - ❏ Learning vocabulary
   - ❏ Listening
   - ❏ Practice tests
   - ❏ Reading
   - ❏ Speaking

5 How would you evaluate your level in each of the following? (1 = beginner
   2 = intermediate 3 = advanced)
   - ❏ Conversation
   - ❏ Grammar
   - ❏ Listening
   - ❏ Reading
   - ❏ Writing
   - ❏ Pronunciation
   - ❏ Vocabulary

6 What have you found most useful to you in your language learning?
   ....
   ....
   ....

From *Learning One-to-One* © Cambridge University Press 2010   PHOTOCOPIABLE

Box 3.3: Desired outcomes questionnaire

Student's name .... Date ....

1 What is your main reason for learning English?

....

2 What do you use English for now?

....

3 Give some examples of situations where you have to use English.

....

....

4 What do you want to use English for in the future?

....

5 Give some examples of materials (books, films or other materials) you want to understand in English.

....

....

6 What topics do you want to talk about in our lessons? List at least three.

....

....

....

7 What do you (mostly) want to practise in our lessons? Rank from most (=1) to least important.
   - ❑ Grammar
   - ❑ Listening
   - ❑ Pronunciation
   - ❑ Reading
   - ❑ Speaking
   - ❑ Vocabulary
   - ❑ Writing

8 What do you think will help you most to improve your grammar / listening / pronunciation / reading / speaking / vocabulary / writing (choose three)?
   1 ....
   2 ....
   3 ....

Box 3.4: Learning style questionnaire

Student's name .... Date ....

What is your preferred learning style?

1 I prefer to learn by . . .
   a) hearing examples and saying them aloud.
   b) drawing things on paper and organizing them in a chart or diagram.
   c) trying something out and then analysing what I've done.

2 When I learn a new grammar point . . .
   a) I like to hear how it's used in conversation.
   b) I like to see lots of examples first.
   c) I try to use it right away.

3 I remember new phrases best when I . . .
   a) repeat them several times.
   b) write them in my notebook.
   c) imagine myself using them in a situation.

4 If I went to an English-speaking country, I would most enjoy . . .
   a) hearing the language used in different contexts.
   b) seeing the language around me.
   c) trying to do things in the language.

5 If I don't understand something, I will . . .
   a) ask the teacher to explain.
   b) try to show the teacher what I don't understand.
   c) try to do the task over again.

6 For language learning, I would most enjoy . . .
   a) listening to music and the radio.
   b) looking at photographs or watching films.
   c) doing activities such as visiting a shop or a museum.

7 In my one-to-one lessons, I want to . . .
   a) learn by listening to real English.
   b) look at interesting materials.
   c) learn to be more interactive in my conversation.

Count up your answers.   a) .... b) .... c) ....
Mostly a)s = auditory learning style; mostly b)s = visual learning style; mostly c)s = kinesthetic learning style. Most people have a blend of learning styles.

From *Learning One-to-One* © Cambridge University Press 2010   PHOTOCOPIABLE

Box 3.5: Your job questionnaire

Student's name .... Date ....

What is your job? ....

What is your job title? ....

Where do you work? ....

How long have you worked there? ....

What are your job responsibilities? ....

....

How much time do you spend using English every day?

....

What tasks do you do in English? ....

....

....

I need English to talk to ....

Which of the following do you need to do in English in your job? Rank from most
(=1) to least important.
- ❑ Give instructions
- ❑ Give presentations
- ❑ Make appointments
- ❑ Negotiate agreements
- ❑ Sell products
- ❑ Socialize
- ❑ Speak on the phone
- ❑ Take part in meetings
- ❑ Talk to colleagues at meetings and conferences
- ❑ Understand instructions
- ❑ Write and read emails
- ❑ Write reports
- ❑ Read articles, reports, contracts
- ❑ Others ....

Box 3.6: Your interests questionnaire

Student's name .... Date ....

My hobbies and interests are . . .	
In my free time, I like to . . .	
I like to listen to . . .	
I enjoy reading . . .	
I enjoy talking about . . .	

From *Learning One-to-One* © Cambridge University Press 2010   PHOTOCOPIABLE

Box 3.7: Wants and needs questionnaire

Student's name .... Date ....

What do you want to be able to do in English?
What do you need to do in English (for your job)?

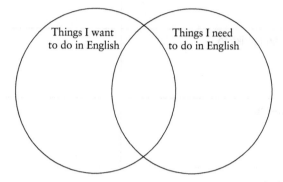

Things I want
to do in English

Things I need
to do in English

From *Learning One-to-One* © Cambridge University Press 2010   PHOTOCOPIABLE

Box 3.8: Job skills and tasks questionnaire

Student's name... Date ....

a) How important are each of these English skills in your job?

reading / writing / speaking / listening

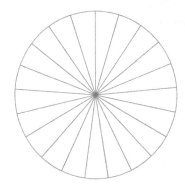

b) What kinds of language practice do you think will help you most to improve your English?

reading / writing / speaking / listening / grammar / pronunciation / vocabulary

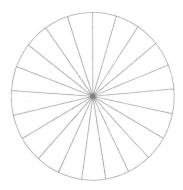

Box 3.9: Lesson planning questionnaire

Student's name .... Date ....

What percentage (%) of time in each lesson do you want to spend on each language skill/area?

1 I want to spend .... % of the lesson on speaking.

2 I want to spend .... % of the lesson on listening.

3 I want to spend .... % of the lesson on reading.

4 I want to spend .... % of the lesson on writing.

5 I want to spend .... % of the lesson on vocabulary.

6 I want to spend .... % of the lesson on pronunciation.

7 I want to spend .... % of the lesson on grammar.

8 I want to spend .... % of the lesson on ....

9 Please fill out the diagram with portions labelled according to your ideal lesson.

10 I want to spend some lessons on . . .
- ❏ work-related topics
- ❏ literature
- ❏ current affairs
- ❏ cultural topics
- ❏ other ....

Note: this information could also be recorded in the form of a pie chart.

From *Learning One-to-One* © Cambridge University Press 2010   PHOTOCOPIABLE

Summary
- There are many different aspects of learners' needs that can help you plan your course.
- Learner needs can change and evolve as your course progresses.
- Needs analyses can be given in a variety of formats and can be used periodically.

- Explain the reason for the needs analysis to your student and what you will do with this information.
- Experiment with a variety of formats in order to obtain a holistic view of your learner's needs, hopes, goals, expectations, learning style, personality.

Course design

Reflection
Think back to the last language course you taught. Was the course based mainly on grammar, functions, skills or a combination? Did your students have a lot of input on the content of the course design?

The various kinds of needs analysis outlined in the previous section will form part of an ongoing process in the development of a unique, individualized course for your student. You might postpone the beginning of the course design phase until you and your student have got to know each other better, or until you have obtained more data from your needs analyses. You will also have to make decisions about the content and organization of the course based on your professional evaluation of your student's needs. Will your course be organized mainly around grammar topics, or around situations at work? Or will you focus on speaking and listening skills with just a small proportion of your time being allotted to grammar and vocabulary?

In some cases, the course design will be determined by external sources. You might be teaching for a language school that has predetermined course materials or exams. When teaching in a company setting, it will be essential to provide the sponsor or employer with a clear outline of your course design and objectives. If you are co-teaching with other tutors, it will be even more important to have a consistent course design in order to coordinate your efforts. Even if you are following a coursebook syllabus, however, you will probably find it necessary to supplement and adapt it to the needs of your learner. In most cases, your course design will be the result of a process of negotiation between you and your student.

One of the advantages of one-to-one learning is that the student can have a significant level of input into the content and design of the course. If you choose to work collaboratively with your student on a course design, it is important to remember that not all students will be sympathetic to a collaborative approach. Many students will feel that it is the teacher's responsibility to design the course. However, trying to fulfil this expectation by shouldering the responsibility for all the planning may result in disappointment for a number of different reasons. First, it does not take advantage of the unique opportunities afforded by one-to-one for personalized learning. Second, the teacher's vision of what the student needs may be significantly different from the student's reality. Third, if the student is not engaged in the process of designing the course content, and does not have the added stimulus of input from peer students, they will be more likely to lose motivation and drop out. (Please see the suggestions in the next sections for some ways to collaborate with your student in the design of your course.) It is a good idea, therefore, to discuss the reasons for your choice of course design, show how you have related it to the information you obtained in your needs analysis and explain the reasons why you are asking for your student's input.

Another factor to consider is negotiating goals for your course that are realistic and achievable. You might want to clarify quite early on in the course that significant language improvement requires hard work both in and out of class and to discuss exactly what aspects of language the student wants to achieve significant progress in.

Finally, even with one-to-one teaching that is very informal, it is important to build in the opportunity for ongoing as well as final evaluation so that progress can be measured and motivation maintained. In more formal contexts, when the student is sponsored by their employer, stakeholders will expect regular reports on their progress. In such cases, it is essential to give your learner every opportunity to practise the test tasks and understand the evaluative criteria. Keep careful records of all test scores. One-to-one also offers the advantage of being able to give personalized feedback on test performance and discuss test-taking strategies with your student.

Planning your course

Below are some suggestions for ways to work together with your student to plan your course. This type of collaborative planning requires the active participation of your student, so if you choose to plan your course in this way, take time to explain the purpose and value of this approach and make sure that your student agrees.

A topic-based course plan

One way to approach your course design is to plan your lessons around the topics your student needs and wants to talk about, drawing on information from your earlier needs analysis. For beginning-level students, these may be very general topics, such as shopping, food or sport. For higher-level students, they may include topics such as the environment, fashion or politics. Here is one idea for engaging your student in planning this type of course.

Write the names of the topics on sticky notes (or use pictures for younger learners). Have some blank sticky notes available so that you or your student can suggest additional topics. Then prepare a grid with squares marked out with dates for your next lessons on a poster or on your interactive whiteboard (see *Box 3.10*). In your lesson, read through the topics with your student one by one, and ask your student to arrange them on the grid according to their importance or interest. Keep the list of sticky notes in a transparent plastic sleeve and make a copy of the grid for your student. Refer to it later for periodic updating.

If you are following a grammar-based course (see below), these topics could be used to supplement your grammar lessons, perhaps used as a conversation starter at the beginning or end of each lesson. The advantage of getting your student to keep a record of this list is that you can ask them to prepare a short talk, or bring in a picture or an article on the topic ahead of time.

Box 3.10: A plan for a topic-based course

Monday 5 August	Monday 12 August	Monday 19 August	Monday 26 August	Monday 2 September
food	shopping	sport	free-time activities	music

A grammar-based course plan

Another way to approach your course design is to plan your lessons around the grammar topics your student needs to work on. You may have already identified some of these through your earlier needs analysis. Here is one idea for engaging your student in planning this type of course.

Select some examples of your student's written work that you have already corrected and select some frequent errors to fill in the first column of an error analysis worksheet such as the one in *Box 3.11*. (This is easier to do if your student submits work by email.) You could also use a transcript of your student's spoken work.

Box 3.11: Error analysis worksheet

Error	Grammar point	Impor-tance	Difficulty	Date practised

This idea is adapted from *Treatment of Error in Second Language Student Writing* by Dana R. Ferris, The University of Michigon Press 2002.

From *Learning One-to-One* © Cambridge University Press 2010   PHOTOCOPIABLE

Using your student's examples as a guide, discuss the types of errors found in their work with them and ask them to write the relevant grammar point in the second column. Add any other grammar points that your student feels they need more practice with.

Number the types of errors from most to least important. (Do they impede comprehension in speaking? Do they cause misunderstandings?) You could also discuss level of difficulty as some might need several lessons. Keep a copy of this sheet, and give one to your student. Review it periodically to check off what has been covered, what needs more work or to add more topics.

As mentioned in *Chapter 2* (pp. 21–5), your student's personality and attitude to error correction will determine how effective this approach will be. It may be most useful for students who do not see the need for grammar practice. Intensive analysis of errors, on the other hand, could be discouraging for students who lack confidence. Another approach is to identify those errors that are caused mainly by L1 transfer. (A useful book for this purpose is *Learner English: A Teacher's Guide to Interference and Other Problems* (Second edition) edited by Michael Swan and Bernard Smith, Cambridge University Press 2001.) This may help to counter the possible negative effect of over-focusing on errors.

A function-based course plan

Another way to design your course to match the needs of your student is to look at what they need to do with the language. Do they need to know how to give instructions, for example, or how to make suggestions and give advice? Here is one idea for engaging your student in planning this type of course.

Make a list of functions and examples of their exponents and write each one on a separate card (see *Box 3.12* on p. 54). Functions and examples can be written in different coloured pens. Go through the cards with your student one by one, and ask your student to arrange them in order of usefulness in everyday conversation or in their job. Ask for some real-life examples of the contexts and situations in which your student uses these functions in their job. Keep a record of the responses and refer to it when you are choosing functions for future lessons, noting which ones you have covered and how often, as in the error analysis worksheet (*Box 3.11*) above.

It may help to look at the table of contents of one or two coursebooks that have a functional syllabus, to give students an idea of the concept of 'functions' as opposed to 'grammar exponents'. Functions generally include a mixture of structures, but this may not be immediately apparent to your student. One of the benefits of this activity is that students will understand your aims better when you introduce a communicative type of lesson rather than focusing on a single grammatical structure.

Setting goals (1)

Goal setting is another way to engage your student in the design of your course. Encouraging your student to set their own goals for learning will help them to become more self-directed and maintain their motivation.

First, discuss with your student the importance of setting goals. (They help you measure progress and direct your own learning.) You might want to give some examples of work or study goals (getting a promotion, passing an exam). A realistic goal should be concrete, personal and achievable. For example, 'improve my writing' is quite vague, but 'write emails for work' is more concrete. Give some examples of different types of language learning goals and the steps needed to achieve them (see *Box 3.13* on p. 54).

Box 3.12: Functions and language examples

Functions	Examples	Functions	Examples
Ask for advice	What should I do? How can I solve this problem?	**Ask for permission**	Can I / May I close the window?
Give advice	You should/ had better/ ought to go home.	**Express regrets**	I wish I hadn't stayed out late last night. / If only I had listened more carefully.
Give directions	Go straight ahead and take the first on the left.	**Talk about imaginary situations**	What would you do if you were a millionaire?
Make requests	Could you help me / Would you mind helping me with this box?	**Describe past habits**	I used to play the piano. / I would practise every morning before school.
Give warnings	If you're not careful, you'll cut yourself. / Be careful, otherwise you'll hurt your hand.	**Talk about rules**	You must turn off your cellphone. / You're not allowed to talk in here. / You can't talk here.

✁

From *Learning One-to-One* © Cambridge University Press 2010 　　PHOTOCOPIABLE

Box 3.13: Example goals

Level	Beginner
Goal 1	*Order food in a restaurant*
Why?	*This is important when I travel to the UK or the USA.*
Steps	*1 learn vocabulary for food* *2 learn useful phrases and practise conversations* *3 read menus*

Level	Intermediate
Goal	*Take notes from lectures*
Why?	*This is important when I go to study at university in England.*
Steps	*1 learn some techniques for note-taking in English* *2 learn vocabulary that will come up in my lectures* *3 practise listening and finding the key information*

Level	Advanced
Goal	*Read technical reports*
Why?	*This is important in my job and to get a promotion.*
Steps	*1 learn some techniques for rapid reading in English* *2 learn useful phrases and vocabulary that will come up in reports* *3 practise reading and summarizing reports*

Help your student to identify their own goals by working with them to fill out a worksheet. You can use the one in *Box 3.14* on p. 56 or design your own. Or do one goal together and ask them to complete the others for homework.

Box 3.14: Setting goals

Student's name.. Date ....

My goals

My first goal is ....

Why is this goal important?

....

What are three steps I need to take to reach this goal?

1 ....

2 ....

3 ....

My second goal is ....

Why is this goal important?

....

What are three steps I need to take to reach this goal?

1 ....

2 ....

3 ....

My third goal is ....

Why is this goal important?

....

What are three steps I need to take to reach this goal?

1 ....

2 ....

3 ....

From *Learning One-to-One* © Cambridge University Press 2010   PHOTOCOPIABLE

Setting goals (2)

Another way to set goals is to use the language competence descriptors developed for the Common European Framework of Reference for Languages (CEFR). These descriptors outline what students will be able to do at the end of a course, but they can also be used to set language goals.

You will need to print out a selection of language competencies that are appropriate for your learner. These can be taken from the CEFR (they may need to be simplified and adapted). Write or print each one on a separate card. *Box 3.15* offers some (simplified) examples taken from the CEFR list of descriptors: www.coe.int/T/DG4/Portfolio/?L=E&M=/documents_intro/Data_bank_descriptors.html.

Box 3.15: Language competency descriptors

Beginner–elementary

I can introduce myself and say what I do.

I can give personal information (address, telephone number, nationality, age, family and hobbies).

I can describe myself, my family and other people I know.

I can say what I usually do at home, at university, in my free time.

I can follow simple directions, e.g. how to get from X to Y, by foot or public transport.

I can describe technical equipment or work routines at my place of work.

I can explain simply how to use an apparatus or a machine.

Intermediate–advanced

I can narrate a story or relate the plot of a film or book.

I can understand presentations, demonstrations and lectures which directly or indirectly relate to my vocational field without difficulty.

I can understand announcements and messages on concrete and abstract topics spoken in standard dialect at normal speed.

I can understand a wide range of recorded and broadcast audio material.

Go through the language competencies one by one, asking the learner to place them into one of three piles – yes, no or not sure – and to discuss the reasons as they do so. Having selected a number of 'yes' goals, go through and sort them into two more piles: short term and long term. Finally, encourage the learner to think of any personal objectives that are not yet represented in the 'yes' list and add them to the list. Keep a record of the final list for periodic review and updating.

Setting goals (3)
A third approach to setting goals, which also helps students to become more self-directed in their learning and to participate actively, is to use a learning contract (Knowles 1986). This entails students' more detailed reflection on how to measure their own progress and may work better if it builds on a previous lesson on identifying goals.

You will need a copy of a worksheet for a learning contract (see *Box 3.16*) adapted for the level of your learner. Work together on completing one row, and then ask your student to add more goals and complete one or two rows for homework. Make copies for yourself and refer to them as you plan your course. Review the contract at regular intervals.

Summary
- Use your needs analysis data to design your course.
- Course design is an ongoing process of negotiation with your student.
- Encourage your student to give input on the course design.
- Explain the reason for using a collaborative approach.
- Set goals with your student that are realistic and appropriate.
- Build in regular opportunities to evaluate progress and keep careful records of test scores so that students themselves and other stakeholders are able to see their progress.

Box 3.16: A learning contract

What are you going to learn? (What are your learning goals?)	How are you going to learn? (What kinds of strategies and resources will you use?)	What is your date for achieving this goal?	How will you evaluate whether you have achieved this goal?	What will you be able to do after achieving this goal?
1 To increase my reading speed for reading academic articles.	I'm going to read one article every week, time myself, and write a summary of the main points.	four months	I will keep a record of my reading speed for each article.	I'll be able to read articles more quickly and keep up to date with developments in my field.
2				
3				

From *Learning One-to-One* © Cambridge University Press 2010   PHOTOCOPIABLE

Lesson planning

> **Reflection**
> *What is your ideal one-to-one lesson? Is it one that is carefully planned, or one that flows naturally from one phase to another?*

- 'I generally like to start off with a conversational topic and use that to lead into the main grammar point of the lesson, so the focus of the language comes from my student.'
- 'I usually prepare a lesson plan, using real news articles, and plan out the vocabulary and grammar, so at the end of the lesson, my student has a clear idea of what we studied.'
- 'I like lessons where my student does most of the talking and I just intervene when they get stuck for a word.'
- 'My student seems to prefer lessons where we follow the book and just chat a bit around the edges. I think it gives a feeling of security to know that we covered the book.'

Your first lesson

You will probably spend most of your first lesson finding out about your student. You might be using your own version of a needs analysis questionnaire adapted to your context. Your first lesson can often be the one that is most informative for both you and your student. Within just a few minutes, you will know if your student is talkative or quiet, shy or confident, a relaxed learner or a perfectionist. In their turn, your student will also find out what kind of teacher you are: whether you talk a lot, talk quickly, correct every mistake and so on.

It may be that even though your first lesson is one where you are both getting to know each other, you will also need to have a variety of different types of short activities on hand that will help you plan your future lessons. For intermediate students, you might choose a short dictation or a short writing task, a mini role play or a short talk. All of these tasks can give you information about your student's language level and learning preferences. You will play the role of 'observer', possibly taking notes of frequent errors, helpful personal information, and seeing which kinds of activities they are familiar with and enjoy.

Think about recording this lesson. The reason for this is that you can use this as a baseline against which to compare your student's future language performance. If you ask your student to give a short talk on their favourite hobby, for example, this would be an excellent task to compare again later in your course. This can come in very useful if you reach a stage when your student feels they are not making much progress.

Planning your lesson: aims

The aims for any single lesson will be determined by the course goals you have chosen with your student (see previous section). Here are some examples:

- to practise the simple past
- to learn vocabulary about holidays
- to read some holiday ads
- to improve confidence in speaking
- to improve pronunciation of past tense forms.

From your point of view, it is important to know what these aims are and to clarify them by writing them down before the lesson (at least for the first few lessons or when you are trying out new material). This will help you to avoid getting sidetracked and enable you to respond flexibly to your student, while still focusing on the lesson aims.

From your student's point of view, it is probably enough to choose one or two of the main aims. Presenting these at the start of your lesson will help your student to focus their attention and to understand where the lesson is heading. Some students respond well to a detailed 'big picture' approach. For example:

> Today we're going to practise the simple past, learn some vocabulary about holidays and read some holiday ads. We'll spend about 15 minutes on the grammar, 20 minutes on vocabulary and speaking, and 15 minutes on reading. Does that sound good?

It might help to have these aims written down on a card or displayed on a screen so that you can refer to them as you progress through the lesson. They will help you to recap what you have done at the end of the lesson, and you can also combine this with getting some instant feedback. For example:

> Today we practised the simple past, learned some vocabulary about holidays and read some holiday ads. We'll review them in our next lesson. Now which part of the lesson did you find most difficult / easiest / most interesting, etc.? Which part do you think we need to go over again?

Being clear about your agenda at the start of the lesson and recapping at the end of the lesson are two ways of providing structure to your lesson, even one that seemingly consisted of a single seamless conversation. It lets your student know that you are thinking about the overall plan of the course and makes them aware of the lesson aims even though they may not have been aware of them while the lesson was going on.

There are more suggestions for getting feedback from your learner in *Chapter 5*.

Planning your lesson: tasks and activities

As well as writing down the aims of your lesson, it is worth taking some time to write a brief summary of the steps of your lesson and how long each step will take. This will probably only be an outline, as the benefit of one-to-one is that you can be completely flexible.

Your outline for a 60-minute lesson could look something like this:

1 Warm-up: chat about last weekend (5 minutes).
2 Go over previous homework (5 minutes).
3 Pre-teach vocabulary about holidays using pictures (10 minutes).
4 Ask and tell about last holiday (15 minutes).
5 Identify past tense verbs used by student and make a list (2 minutes).
6 Brief drill practice on past tense forms (1 minute).
7 Grammar worksheet about past tense (10 minutes)
   (short break – 2 minutes).
8 Read ads about holidays and make a list of new vocabulary
   (5 minutes).
9 Role play conversation with someone who went on one of these
   holidays (5 minutes).
10 Recap and give homework (write about last holiday)
   Extra activity: guessing game about famous places.

Another idea is to map out your plan in the form of a pie chart like the one in *Box 3.17*. This can give a clearer impression of the balance and relative timing of the different stages.

Box 3.17: Lesson plan in the form of a pie chart

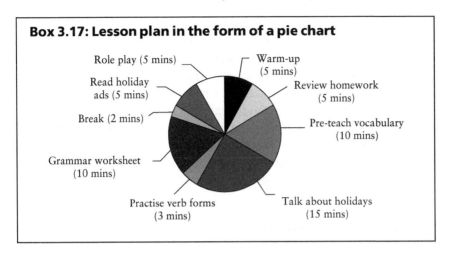

Role play (5 mins)
Read holiday ads (5 mins)
Break (2 mins)
Grammar worksheet (10 mins)
Practise verb forms (3 mins)
Warm-up (5 mins)
Review homework (5 mins)
Pre-teach vocabulary (10 mins)
Talk about holidays (15 mins)

Making a plan will help you see if you have included a variety of activity types, a variety of teacher roles, time for your student to talk about personal information, time to build on what your student already knows, and some extra activities in case you run out of material. It is usually a good idea to have a back-up plan, too, just in case – for whatever reason – this plan turns out to be inappropriate. Let us say, for example, that you planned a lesson on food, but then found out that your student is on a weight-loss diet at the moment and food is the last thing they want to talk about.

Having a plan does not mean, however, that you have to stick to it rigidly. The beauty of one-to-one is that you can improvise at a moment's notice and with very little preparation, if you notice a pronunciation point that needs work, for example, or discover a topic that grabs your or your student's interest.

Collaborative lesson planning

Engaging your student's collaboration in your lesson planning is also something that a one-to-one teacher can take advantage of. It takes time to learn how to involve your student and create an atmosphere where they feel able to participate actively. Start with easy and manageable tasks such as asking your student to bring in pictures, photos, articles, recommend websites, and to suggest topics and materials for your lesson. You could take turns picking the topics, or you could ask your student to take responsibility for one section of each lesson where they could teach you something, such as an aspect of their language or culture, or something about their job.

A portfolio is another way to engage your learner in the lesson planning process. A portfolio (either book-style, or online in the form of a blog) can serve a variety of different functions, such as helping to record your learner's progress and providing a sense of achievement. It is also a useful tool for identifying objectives for future lessons. Finally, it also helps your learner to develop skills of self-evaluation (as they are the ones who decide what should go into the portfolio), which are essential to independent learning. See *Box 3.18* for an example of a way to work with your student on planning your portfolio. You can find detailed information related to the European Language Portfolio on the Council of Europe website (www.coe.int/T/DG4/Portfolio).

Box 3.18: Your portfolio

A portfolio can help me in my learning because . . .
> . . . it is a record of my learning progress.
> . . . it is a place to keep work that I am proud of.
> . . . it is a place to keep useful examples of:

- ❑ Letters
- ❑ Forms
- ❑ Descriptions
- ❑ Poems
- ❑ Songs
- ❑ Recipes
- ❑ Wordlists
- ❑ Postcards
- ❑ Emails
- ❑ Essays
- ❑ Books I have read
- ❑ Films I have seen
- ❑ Selected journal entries
- ❑ Samples of creative writing
- ❑ ....
- ❑ ....
- ❑ ....

I will show my portfolio to:

❑ my teacher ❑ my boss ❑ my family ❑ my friends

You can also collaborate on planning a reading programme by choosing a book or a reader for your student to read in their free time and which you can use for lesson activities. Bring in a selection of readers (see Cambridge Readers website, www.cambridge.org/ELT/READERS) if available, or visit a library together and choose one that is appropriate in level and content. Set aside regular times to discuss the story and base activities around it. Use a reading log and book report (see *Box 3.19* and *Box 3.20* on p. *66*) to help your student chart their progress, the new words they have learned and their opinions of the books.

Box 3.19: Reading log

Title and author	Date read	How long (pages)	My opinion

From *Learning One-to-One* © Cambridge University Press 2010   PHOTOCOPIABLE

Box 3.20: Book report

Title and author	....
Setting (time and place)	....
Main characters	....
Main story	....
Conclusion of story	....
Useful key words and phrases	....
My opinion	....

Finally, a great advantage of one-to-one is that you can actually learn and practise English by doing things together, such as cooking a dish by following a recipe, learning a board game, learning how to do something online (e.g. create a wiki or a collaborative multimedia project online) or visiting a museum, an art gallery or a zoo (in the real world or in the virtual world). These active 'learning by doing' lessons can give your student a chance to contribute to the learning process (see *Activity 10.4: Give a guided tour*). They can provide a lot of material for pre- and post-activities, as well as material for journals and portfolios.

Summary
- Be clear about your lesson aims.
- Tell your student the aims at the start and review them at the end of the lesson.
- Prepare a written plan which is also flexible.
- Include a variety of activities and time for breaks.
- Engage your student in the lesson planning process.

Conclusion

This chapter has given an overview of how to approach needs analysis, course design and lesson planning in the context of one-to-one teaching. It has suggested using a variety of approaches to needs analysis, so that you can build up a holistic picture of your student's language needs, and a collaborative approach to course design and lesson planning so that you can involve your student more actively in the learning process. Lesson planning is an area where there is a need to strike a balance between structure and flexibility. Lessons should be structured enough to provide a sense of direction, but flexible enough to allow space for you and your student to react spontaneously to the needs of the moment, creating a learning interaction that is both purposeful and enjoyable.

4   Selecting and adapting materials

Working together with one student gives you the opportunity to collaborate on choosing and creating learning materials. If you are working in a language school setting with a pre-defined set of course materials, your opportunities may be fewer. Nevertheless, one-to-one teaching is the ideal context for selecting materials (both published ELT materials and authentic materials) that are suited to your student's individual needs and for making more use of learner-selected and learner-generated materials.

This chapter offers some general guidelines for selecting materials and ideas for using learner-generated materials. It also provides some practical examples of how to adapt published ELT materials for one-to-one teaching.

Selecting materials

> *Reflection*
> *Think about a one-to-one lesson that worked really well. What kinds of materials did you use? Why did it work well?*

When choosing materials for your lesson, you may find it helpful to consider the following questions:

- *Why did I choose the material?* What interested me about it? Why do I think it will interest my student? Does it reflect their learning style? Is it visually appealing?
- *Is it relevant to my student's goals?* Which goals? What will it help them do?
- *What is my teaching purpose in using this material?* Does the material contain any useful language features (e.g. collocations, discourse markers, idioms) that could be focused on?
- *Will most of the vocabulary be familiar?* Which words or sections will be easy or difficult for my student? How will we tackle the unfamiliar words?
- *Is it culturally appropriate?* Is there any cultural information that my student will learn from this material or will need in order to understand it? Is there any cultural aspect that might be sensitive or offensive?

- *What problems might come up when using this material?* Could there be too much new vocabulary, or is the material too long to finish in one lesson? What solutions can I think of to these problems ahead of time?
- *Does the material provide opportunities for supplementing and extending if necessary?* Can it lead into a role play or a homework task? Can we look up related information on the internet?

Noting down your reflections will also help you organize your ideas and thoughts in a more disciplined and productive way. This may be in the form of a brief note or reminder to yourself about lessons you have taught or will teach, or something more systematic, as in *Box 4.1* on p. 70, which shows an example of a teacher's reflections on the choice of materials for an individual student.

This kind of written reflection can help you to clarify your assumptions and form part of your ongoing professional development (see *Chapter 5* for more ideas on reflection).

Learner-selected materials

Advanced-level students will probably have a better idea of what kinds of materials will help them study best. Lower-level students can sometimes be over-ambitious in their hopes of what they can achieve. Try offering them a choice of a limited number of options and asking them to choose one for the next lesson. This can be done in a number of different ways. For example:

- Bring a selection of three or four articles (from a newspaper, magazine or the internet) and choose the most interesting one.
- Bring a selection of three or four easy readers and choose one for extensive reading.
- Go through the coursebook or supplementary book you have selected and choose which units to study.
- Read through the table of contents of a coursebook or supplementary book and select the most the interesting and useful topics.
- Bring a selection of pictures (from magazines or postcards) and use them to choose which topic to discuss.
- Ask your student to choose one paragraph of an article or a textbook for intensive study.
- Email your student a choice of three or four websites and ask them to decide which one you will discuss and study in your next lesson.

Box 4.1: A teacher's notebook entry

Material chosen	Newspaper article about downsizing companies by outsourcing overseas.
Why did I choose the material?	It's topical at the moment and in the news a lot. Up-to-date topic and information which my student will have opinions about.
Is it relevant to my student's goals?	Useful vocabulary related to my student's job as Human Resources manager.
What is my teaching purpose in using this material?	To help my student develop and express arguments for and against this topic, and learn vocabulary associated with it.
Will most of the vocabulary be familiar?	A lot of difficult vocabulary. I'll have to pre-teach some of the key terminology.
Is it culturally appropriate?	Article assumes that the reader will disagree with moving jobs overseas, but my student is actively involved in this. Might be offended?
What problems might come up when using this material?	It's a bit long. I might have to choose one section. There are a lot of new words (need to identify the most difficult ones). Student may not agree with the opinion in the article and find it boring or too superficial (need to think of activities to balance the ideas in the article).
Does the material provide opportunities for supplementing and extending if necessary?	We can do a role play based on the article, or write a letter to the paper presenting the opposite point of view, or list out the arguments for and against and practise agreeing and disagreeing.

Some ideas for engaging your student in the process of selecting and finding materials for your lessons may be found in *Part 2* (see, e.g., *Activity 10.5: Cooking lesson*).

Learner-generated materials

As well as helping to select and find materials for your lessons, your student is also an excellent source of study materials. Examples of their written work – whether written in class or for homework – and recordings of spoken language or videos can be used in a number of different ways. You could ask your student to bring examples of their work in English, such as letters or emails they have written for work, or an essay they have written for school. You can also keep copies (electronic or print) of their emails to you and use them to work on in your lesson. Some ideas for using learner-generated materials in your lessons may be found in *Part 2* (see, e.g., *Activity 8.1: Correcting written homework*).

Using authentic materials

One-to-one is ideal for using authentic materials as you need only one copy of a piece of reading or writing material (e.g. a newspaper article, a menu, a calendar, a catalogue, a holiday brochure, an application form, a questionnaire, a medical form) and you can plan a whole lesson around it. Authentic materials are motivating because students feel they have tackled real English, but they can also be discouraging if there is too much new vocabulary. However, there are many authentic materials, such as menus and shopping flyers, that can be used even at low levels. Some ideas for using authentic materials in your lessons may be found in *Part 2* (see, e.g., *Activity 10.8: Selling a product*).

Box 4.2 on p. 72 gives an example lesson outline for using some authentic reading material, in this case an article from a magazine.

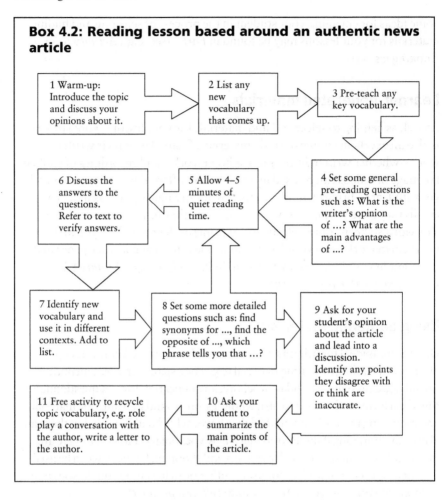

Box 4.2: Reading lesson based around an authentic news article

1 Warm-up: Introduce the topic and discuss your opinions about it.

2 List any new vocabulary that comes up.

3 Pre-teach any key vocabulary.

4 Set some general pre-reading questions such as: What is the writer's opinion of ...? What are the main advantages of ...?

5 Allow 4–5 minutes of quiet reading time.

6 Discuss the answers to the questions. Refer to text to verify answers.

7 Identify new vocabulary and use it in different contexts. Add to list.

8 Set some more detailed questions such as: find synonyms for ..., find the opposite of ..., which phrase tells you that ...?

9 Ask for your student's opinion about the article and lead into a discussion. Identify any points they disagree with or think are inaccurate.

10 Ask your student to summarize the main points of the article.

11 Free activity to recycle topic vocabulary, e.g. role play a conversation with the author, write a letter to the author.

Some general principles for adapting published coursebook materials for one-to-one

Most published materials produced for ELT are intended for classroom use with groups of students. They usually include pair- or group-work activities designed to encourage students to speak with each other. Although following a class coursebook is helpful in structuring your course, it will usually need to be adapted.

Planning

Before your lesson, read through the material, keeping your learner clearly in mind. Anticipate how long you will be likely to spend on each section of the lesson. The time estimate will vary depending on your learner's personality as well as their language level. Activities intended for group and pair work can often take longer to complete in a group class setting than when working with an individual. Decide on your focus for each part of the lesson and which sections of the lesson you feel will be of most benefit to your learner or could possibly be skipped. Identify which parts of the lesson are likely to need extra support or extra practice material.

Personalization

Choose materials that can be adapted to have personal relevance to your individual student, to their job or to their culture. One-to-one learning offers multiple opportunities to make language learning more meaningful (and therefore more motivating and memorable) by adapting the material to the individual's interests, but many classroom materials are intentionally very general in order to appeal to the widest range of possible interests. In one-to-one, you can focus your attention on any specific aspect of a topic that your student finds interesting and skip the less interesting aspects.

Role reversal

Whenever you have materials that require the student to answer questions about themselves, or about the target culture, there is also an opportunity for the student to use the same questions to interview you about yourself, your job and your culture (or another culture you know well). This is a natural information gap, and you can use it to play the role of conversation partner and focus on communication.

Modelling

For exercises that are difficult or unfamiliar, it is sometimes easier to show your student what you want them to do by modelling the task yourself while verbally describing what you are doing (a kind of thinking aloud or verbal protocol). The type of language you use will depend on level, but it is a good way to get students to verbalize their learning strategies too, something that might be too artificial in a large group context. And you may also draw more language out of the material by showing that you want students to find examples in the text to support their answers to a true/false question, or explain why they chose (a) rather than (b) or (c) in a multiple-choice exercise.

Recycling

Exercises and activities tend to take up more lesson time in a group context because you have other students offering multiple possible answers, discussing with each other and exchanging opinions. In one-to-one, there might be a tendency to move too quickly through exercises, feeling perhaps that it is boring for your student to linger too long on one exercise once it is done. This is not necessarily true. One-to-one students benefit greatly from recycling the same material in different ways because they have not had the interactive peer learning that goes on in a classroom. It is therefore important to use activities that recycle the same language in order to allow time for new language to be processed.

Supplementing

In order to make the materials relevant to your learner, you might need to have strategies for making a fluency exercise more structured, for example, or for turning a grammar exercise into a role play, depending on your student's needs and goals. Supplementing does not necessarily mean that you need more materials, but you will need ideas for different ways of using the same materials.

It is also the case that role play and other pair-work activities that are useful practice between two students are not as time-efficient between teacher and student because the teacher does not need an equal amount of practice. In these cases, it is useful to think about additional ideas to extend and expand exercises so that they maximize your student's production of language and minimize your own.

Learner takes control

One-to-one is a wonderful opportunity for the teacher to give up some of the power of decision-making in the lesson. As part of the process of helping your learner to develop independent study skills, you can gradually introduce them to ways of taking control of the lesson to adjust the pace or level, or to choose which direction a discussion will follow. This is much easier to do when teaching one-to-one, as there is no need to compromise between the differing needs of people in a group.

Examples of adapting tasks and exercises in published coursebook materials

Below is a selection of examples of tasks and exercises that might be adapted for use with one-to-one students. I have chosen them because I think they are generic examples of activities and exercises that are frequently found in classroom textbooks and are useful for illustrating the general principles outlined above.

Warm-up/discussion questions

Box 4.3 provides an example of an introductory (warm-up) exercise to a text about international tipping etiquette.

Box 4.3: Example warm-up activity

8C A bit extra

 Work in groups. Discuss these questions.

1 Who do people usually give tips to in your country?
2 How much do people tip them?
3 Why might people decide not to tip them?

© Cambridge University Press 2007

Personalization

The questions in *Box 4.3* provide an interesting starting point for discussion which can lead into a more personalized discussion of your and your student's personal tipping policy. What makes you decide to give a tip, or to give a large tip?

Role reversal

If you and your learner are from different cultures, ask your student to interview you about tipping in your culture, or in another culture that you know well. Ask them to write a few dos and don'ts based on the information. If you are from the same culture, discuss what kind of advice to give to a visitor and make a list.

Supplementing

A learner who enjoys free conversation and talking about personal experiences could easily spend 15–20 minutes on this opening activity. To structure this more, you may decide to record the opening discussion and come back to it for later analysis. A quiet learner may need some extra support here. For example, you could work together to compile a list of situations when you would and would not give a tip. For students who want to focus on vocabulary, you can use this discussion to start making a list (or a mind map) of new words and phrases for this topic that correspond to ideas that your learner wants to express.

Reading comprehension exercises

Box 4.4 provides an example of a reading comprehension exercise for a text about a ghost-hunting weekend (the reading text is not shown).

Modelling

To exploit this exercise more, model an expanded answer to the first question. For example:

> Sentence number one is false because the first sentence in the text says that 1 in 10 claim to have seen a ghost, and that is only 1% of the population.

In other words, first say if the statement is true or false. Then identify the place in the text where you found the information. Finally describe why the sentence supports or contradicts the statement.

Supplementing

There are many ways of checking reading comprehension, but because of space restrictions, the coursebook can provide only a limited number of options. For this reading text, you can add other question types in addition to the true/ false questions in exercise 2c). For example, some open-ended questions (*How many people believe in ghosts?*) or some multiple-choice questions (*Who suggested the ghost-hunting trip, Pat or her sister?*). Another strategy is to allocate a few minutes of quiet reading time when both you and your student can prepare some additional questions about the text either verbally or in writing. (An added challenge is to ask only questions the other has not thought of.)

Box 4.4: Example reading comprehension exercise

Lesson 12C Spooky!

 c) Read the article again. Tick the true sentences. Correct the false ones.

1 More than half the population of the UK say they have seen a ghost.
2 The writer didn't expect to see a ghost at Brockfield Castle.
3 The writer thought most of the other ghost-hunters were strange.
4 The ghosts who haunt the castle are Ashley's brothers.
5 There had been a fire in the room where the writer saw the old man.
6 The writer has changed her mind about the existence of ghosts.

d) Work in pairs. Discuss these questions.

1 What do you think really happened at Brockfield Castle that weekend?
2 Would you like to go on a ghost-hunting weekend? Why?/Why not?

© Cambridge University Press 2007

To focus on note-taking skills, make a flowchart diagram of the events in the story. For students who need fluency practice, role play a conversation between the author of the article and a friend, or role play an interview between the author of the article and a ghost-sceptic. Then switch roles with your student and role play an interview with a ghost-believer.

Learner takes control

Encourage your student to ask about any difficult words or idioms in the text and use this as an opportunity to practise the skill of guessing from context. Use the words they have chosen to create vocabulary cards with example sentences or pictures to use for review next time. Ask your learner to choose a small section of the text for dictation. You can dictate the exact text, or dictate the text with gaps (just say 'beep' or 'gap' for the gaps) which your student will then have to complete, or dictate the text with small changes which your student will have to find.

Personalization

Ask your student if they or their friends have had any supernatural experiences. Talk about attitudes towards ghosts and the supernatural in their culture. How are their personal views similar to or different from those of the people in the story?

Role reversal

Exercise 2d) focuses on personal response to the text and to the topic. To extend this, ask your student to question you about your opinions. Use this opportunity to practise strategies for agreeing and disagreeing politely. Extend the discussion to ask why people in general might like to go on ghost-hunting weekends, or what type of person might be interested in it. Again, it may be useful for your student to interview you about this topic and find out how similar or different your points of view are.

Listening comprehension exercises

Box 4.5 provides an example of a comprehension exercise for a conversation about ghost experiences.

Box 4.5: Example listening comprehension exercise

Lesson 12C Spooky!

Listening

 5 **a)** **R12.7** Listen to a conversation between three friends, Laura, Chris and Mark. What problem does Laura have? What do Chris and Mark think about her problem?

b) Listen again. Make notes on the reasons why Laura thinks she has this problem.

c) Work in pairs. Compare notes. What do you think Laura should do?

© Cambridge University Press 2007

Supplementing

Create (or ask your student to create) additional comprehension questions about the audio. Try to identify the setting and the speakers. Are there any clues to their personality or background? What can you learn from their tone of voice and intonation? Then listen again for vocabulary, write down new words associated with the topic, as well as any words that were repeated from the reading text. Did they have the same meanings or different ones?

Learner takes control

After listening to the whole conversation once, and answering questions 5a) and 5b), you can focus on the sections that seem to cause most difficulty. Ask your student to make notes or raise their hand to signal which sections they would like to hear again. Look at the audio transcript to pick out useful phrases that your student thinks they might use. Ask your student to select some lines of the audio for dictation, language analysis, phonological analysis, intensive practice or repetition. Your learner can take control of the pause button and stop the audio to ask you questions about the content or about grammar and vocabulary.

Recycling

After listening two or three times, role play a conversation between Laura
and another friend, or between Laura and a ghost-hunting specialist where
she explains her problem and the ghost-hunter offers to help.

Modelling

As the first listening exercise focuses on note-taking, you might want to take
notes yourself while you are listening. Either play a short section first and show
your student an example of how to take notes. Or take notes yourself throughout
the whole listening and then compare your notes afterwards with your student
and identify the best points, for example use of numbers, abbreviations, short
forms, leaving out subject pronouns and auxiliary verbs, etc.

Grammar practice exercises

Box 4.6 shows an example of a grammar practice exercise for beginners.

Box 4.6: Example beginner-level grammar practice exercise

2 Practice

Write. Look at the map. Complete the sentences.

1. *A* Where's the park?
   B It's ___*next to*___ the bank.
2. *A* Where's the library?
   B It's _____ the bank.
3. *A* Where's the school?
   B It's _____ First Street
   and Grant Avenue.
4. *A* Where's the hospital?
   B It's _____ Grant Avenue.
5. *A* Where's the bank?
   B It's _____ the school and the park.
6. *A* Where's the post office?
   B It's _____ the library.

© Cambridge University Press 2007

Recycling

After completing the practice exercise, go over it again by saying the answers in random order – your student will identify the buildings. For example:

Teacher: It's next to the bank.
Student: The park.

Switch roles. Your student identifies the locations and you say the names of the places. Repeat the answers again, this time without looking at the questions, only looking at the map. Repeat the questions again, without looking at the questions, only looking at the map. Make yes/no questions about the places on the map. Ask your student to make yes/no questions. Now make some false statements about locations on the map. Your student will correct you.

Personalization

Draw a new map to show some streets in your local neighbourhood. Help your student to draw the map and identify the buildings. Then practise the exercise again using the new places and names.

Supplementing

If your student needs help with fluency, try adding one or two phrases to these exchanges. For example:

Excuse me. Where's the bank?
Could you say that again, please?
Thank you very much.
You're welcome.

Focus on friendly polite intonation.

Learner takes control

Ask your student to 'dictate' a map to you so that you can draw it (asking questions to clarify as you go along). Your student can use this new map to write a set of questions and answers similar to the ones in the book.

Box 4.7 provides an example of an intermediate-level grammar practice exercise.

Box 4.7: Example intermediate-level grammar practice exercise

Write *for* or *since*.

1. Rachel has been in Brazil *since* _____ Monday.
2. Rachel has been in Brazil *for* _____ three days.
3. My aunt has lived in Australia _____ 15 years.
4. Jennifer is in her office. She has been there _____ 7 o'clock.
5. Mexico has been an independent country _____ 1821.
6. The bus is late. We've been waiting _____ 20 minutes.
7. Nobody lives in those houses. They have been empty _____ many years.
8. Luis has been sick _____ a long time. He has been in the hospital _____ October.

© Cambridge University Press 2002

Modelling

Do the first example yourself and explain why you chose *for* or *since* as the answer. (Does it refer to a point of time or a period of time?) Then ask your student to do the same for the other questions. Use a diagram to illustrate the difference visually and point to the diagram as you speak.

Recycling

After completing the practice exercise (but without writing the answers in), go over it again by asking questions about the statements in random order. For example:

Teacher: How long has your aunt lived in Australia?
Student: For 15 years.

Think of three alternate endings for each sentence. For example:

Rachel has been in Brazil since Monday / February / last year / 2007.

Change each sentence from *since* to *for* and vice versa. For example:

Rachel has been in Brazil since Monday. (Today is Wednesday) → She's been in Brazil for three days.

Personalization

Think of alternative (true) beginnings for each sentence, e.g. *I've had a cold since Monday*. You and your student could list the facts out individually in random order (during a few minutes of quiet time) and then try to guess what the correct endings are for each other's facts. For example, your list might be:

been a teacher
lived in Tokyo
had a cold.

Then your student would guess:

Have you been a teacher for 15 years?
Have you lived in Tokyo since October?
Have you had a cold since Monday?

This could lead into your student creating a personal timeline for extended practice.

Pair-work activities

Box 4.8 provides an example of a pair-work activity.

Box 4.8: Example pair-work activity

a) Work on your own. Make questions with *you* with these words. Use *How long ...?* or *How much/many ...?* and the Present Perfect Simple or Present Perfect Continuous. Use the continuous form if possible.

1 / countries / visit ?
   How many countries have you visited?
2 / live / in your house or flat?
3 / phone calls / make / today?
4 / study / English?
5 / know / your oldest friend?
6 / spend / on food today?

b) Work with your partner. Take turns to ask and answer the questions. Ask follow-up questions.

© Cambridge University Press 2007

Modelling

Answer the first question and show that you want your student to add two or three sentences of extra information to each answer. For example:

> I have visited five countries. India was the most interesting. I've been there twice.

Encourage your student to respond with additional questions. You could also model giving vague answers to the questions. For example, *not many, not very long, quite a few, less than usual*, etc.

Recycling

Give the answers in random order and guess the question. Make small changes to the questions. Answer the questions as another person. Make some quiz questions based on the information you have given. For example:

> I've known my best friend for ten years – true or false?
> False. You've known her for fifteen years.

Ask your student to ask you the questions again, this time turning them into yes/no questions or tag questions. For example:

> A: Have you visited many countries?
> B: Not many / Quite a few.
> A: You've visited a lot of countries, haven't you?
> B: Not really.

Learner takes control

Ask your student to choose the most interesting question and extend it to a longer discussion. If it seems particularly motivating, it could become the basis for a written assignment or journal entry.

Internet-based exercises

Box 4.9 provides an example of an internet-based activity about holiday celebrations around the world.

Box 4.9: Example internet activity

Internet activity

Use the internet to find out about traditional celebrations in another country, for example Mardi Gras, Obon, Inti Raymi and Songkran. Work in groups and share information about each festival. Which website provided the best information about each one?

Modelling

If you have access to the internet during your lesson, you can start off by brainstorming a number of keywords that might bring up useful sites. While you are trying them out together, think aloud through your process of sifting through websites to choose the ones that look most useful and reliable. Ask your student to do the same. If you do not have access to the internet, you can print out a list of web links for one of the topics (with brief descriptions, as they show up on a search engine) and decide which ones are best. Then ask your student to do the same for the other topics for homework.

Reverse roles

Ask your student to look up websites for homework and prepare a questionnaire for you based on one website. They can send it to you by email. In the next lesson, you can go over the questions and the answers together (correcting if necessary). Add further questions about the topic that were not answered on that website. Brainstorm ways of finding out this additional information. Compare findings and research methods in the next lesson.

Personalization

Ask your student to choose a website that is about a celebration in their country. Ask them to critique the website, correcting any false or misleading information and explaining why the information is wrong. Work together to design your own website in electronic or pen-and-paper format. Consider the type of audience you are trying to reach and what you want to tell them.

Recycling

After completing the exercise, use the information to role play an interview with someone from that country. Or compare their celebration with one in your student's country.

Walk around activities

Box 4.10 provides an example of a walk around activity based on adjectives to describe personality.

Box 4.10: Example walk around activity

Group exercise: Write an adjective that describes you on a piece of paper. Give it to your teacher. Your teacher will mix up the papers and give them out again. Walk around the class and ask questions to find the person whose adjective you have.

Modelling

Brainstorm a number of personality adjectives and write each one on a separate piece of paper (e.g. *friendly, quiet, shy, confident, generous*). Spread them out on the table. Ask a question about each word (without using the word) to find out about each characteristic. For example:

> Do you usually give a big tip when you go to a restaurant? (*Answer*: generous)

Your student can make up questions for each of the other words and you will guess which word it is.

Recycling

After completing the exercise, repeat the activity again, this time using only negative sentences, e.g. *I don't usually give a big tip in a restaurant.* You can repeat it again, using opposites or synonyms if appropriate.

Personalization

Ask your student to write five words to describe their own personality and you write ten words to describe yours. Do not show them to each other. Ask questions (without using the target words) to find out how many of the words in your lists are the same. To make this more difficult, write the words in the specific order that you think best describes you and find the correct order.

Role play

Box 4.11 provides an example of a role play activity based on making a complaint in a restaurant.

Box 4.11: Example role play

> **Student A:** You are a server in a restaurant.
> **Student B:** You are a customer in a restaurant. Your coffee is cold. Complain to the server.

Modelling

Before starting the role play, brainstorm some useful phrases that could be used by either person in the role play. For example:

I'd like to make a complaint.
There's a small problem. Could I speak to the manager?
What's the matter? Can I help you?
Is everything all right? etc.

Model appropriate polite intonation for these phrases and ask your student to practise them. Role play the conversation. Then switch roles and role play again, each time modelling additional language that you would like your student to use. Repeat the role play. The conversation should get longer and more fluent every time. When you are ready, record the conversation and listen to it again.

Recycling

Make a list of adjectives to describe the possible feelings or attitudes of people in this role play. For example: *polite, angry, timid, rude, impatient, patient, bossy, nervous, confident, assertive.* Then do the role play in the manner of one of these adjectives (you can try to guess which adjective your partner chose).

Personalization

Discuss what strategies are most acceptable and likely to be successful in your culture or in other cultures that you know. Ask your student to tell you about their experiences of complaining in a restaurant or a shop. Role play the situation they described, using the language you have previously practised.

Conclusion

This chapter has outlined some guidelines for selecting materials and suggested making use of materials that are selected or created by the learner. It has also discussed some general principles for adapting ELT published teaching materials to the one-to-one context. Selecting and adapting materials – whether from authentic or ELT published sources – are an important part of developing lessons that are appropriate for your individual student. Following a coursebook can help to provide an overall structure to your course, but among the main benefits of one-to-one teaching is the freedom to create your own unique, individualized course using materials that are exactly suited to the needs and interests of your learner.

5   **Feedback and reflection**

As one-to-one teaching can vary so much according to the nature of the setting, the learner's aims and needs, as well as their age, culture and personality, it is difficult to set down generalizations about what will or will not work in your lessons. There are, however, two important skills that will help you to adapt your teaching to the demands of any context. The first is the skill of getting useful feedback from your student, and the second is the skill of reflecting on your lessons. Developing these two skills will help to keep your teaching tuned in to the needs of your learner and will also open up pathways for research and exploration that will make your lessons a process of learning not just for your learner, but also for you.

This chapter will offer some suggestions for getting feedback from your student and reflecting on your teaching that will help you tailor your lessons to the needs of your student and develop strategies for your own professional development.

Obtaining student feedback on your lessons

> *Reflection*
> *How often do you ask your student for feedback on your lessons? How do you feel when you ask for feedback? How do you usually use the feedback?*

As with other aspects of learning and teaching, getting feedback is a skill that improves with training and experience. It is important for you to get feedback that will be useful for you. Therefore, a very general question such as *What did you think of today's lesson?* is likely to produce a wide range of answers, many of which may not be at all useful and may even be detrimental to your relationship. A student who says that they did not like the lesson may mean that it was difficult and therefore good, or that this way of learning is new to them, or that the topic was unappealing, or that they felt discouraged by their mistakes. It is best to start by asking for feedback on small, discrete and concrete aspects of the lesson and specify exactly what you want an opinion about. Is it the material, the topic, the level of difficulty or the type of learning activities?

When asking for feedback from your student, it is a good idea to explain why you need it and what you will use it for. You might decide to discuss the feedback in more detail with your student and use it as a starting point to choose future topics and learning activities. If, for whatever reason, you receive negative feedback from your student, always take some time to reflect on the different possible reasons for it and come up with a variety of possible solutions. Your student may not realize how hurtful negative feedback can be for you, and you must be prepared to find ways of turning the negative into positive.

One way of getting feedback is to ask a short question at the end of the lesson or an activity. You can do this very informally and it need not take up a lot of time. After reading an article, you might ask, *What did you like best about the article?* Starting off by asking for a positive response is quite helpful because it leaves space for the student to add something negative if they wish. Learning about the positive aspects of a lesson also helps you to identify the implicit negative aspects. For example, if a student says that they liked the article because it was full of interesting facts, this may tell you that they did not enjoy the fiction story you read the previous week. Also, asking about the material rather than about your teaching makes the discussion less sensitive and personal. When you have achieved a degree of trust with your student, they will be able to speak to you more freely about what things they found most helpful and enjoyable in your lessons.

One problem with verbal feedback is that it can be coloured by emotions and interpretations and, on reflection, can take on different shades of meaning. You can also just forget what was said and, if you have a tendency to be too self-critical, you may remember the negative things more than the positive. Getting written feedback might seem unnecessarily time-consuming but can ultimately help you to avoid long-term problems in any mismatch between your and your student's expectations. Once your student gets used to providing quick written feedback at the end of the lesson, it will take up less time.

Written feedback also means that you do not have to respond immediately and that you have a record to refer to later. You can keep all the slips of paper in a pocket of your folder related to that student and you will gradually be able to build up a picture of your student's learning style and preferences. This will help you to choose materials and design lessons that will enhance your student's learning.

Boxes 5.1a–5.1g offer some suggestions for getting written feedback that is brief, concrete and allows space for students to comment constructively on the teaching/ learning process.

Box 5.1a: Feedback

Name .... Date ....

Today's lesson was about ....

....

Today's lesson was interesting because ....

....

From *Learning One-to-One* © Cambridge University Press 2010   PHOTOCOPIABLE

Box 5.1b: Feedback

Name .... Date ....

Today's lesson was about ....

....

Today's topic was interesting because ....

....

Today's topic was difficult because ....

....

From *Learning One-to-One* © Cambridge University Press 2010   PHOTOCOPIABLE

Box 5.1c: Feedback

Name .... Date ....

Today's lesson was about ....

....

What did you like best about today's lesson? ....

....

Which language practice activity helped you most? ....

....

From *Learning One-to-One* © Cambridge University Press 2010   PHOTOCOPIABLE

Box 5.1d: Feedback

Name .... Date ....

Today's lesson was easy because ....

....

Today's lesson was difficult because ....

....

Which activity in today's lesson would you like to do more of in future lessons?

....

Box 5.1e: Feedback

Name .... Date ....

In today's lesson I enjoyed ....

because ....

....

Box 5.1f: Feedback

Name .... Date ....

What was the most important thing you learned in today's lesson?

....

....

Box 5.1g: Feedback

Name .... Date ....

Today's lesson (choose one or more words for each line below)

easy / difficult / fun / interesting / boring / useful / challenging

Topic   ....
Vocabulary   ....
Discussion   ....
Role play   ....

From *Learning One-to-One* © Cambridge University Press 2010   PHOTOCOPIABLE

Box *5.1h* provides an idea for a colour-coded feedback activity.

You will need coloured sticky dots in at least three different colours. Write the names of the different activities from your lesson on a piece of paper or on your whiteboard (after doing this a few times, you could ask your student to list them). Give your student the coloured dots and explain to them what meaning you have attached to each colour. For example:

Option 1: Red = It was difficult for me; Green = It was useful for me; Yellow = It was fun for me.

Option 2: Red = I listened a lot; Green = I talked a lot; Yellow = I learned a lot.

Option 3: Red = I want to do less of this in class; Green = I want to do more of this in class; Yellow = I want to do this for homework next time.

Tell them that they can put more than one dot on each section. Keep a record of the results for future lesson planning.

Box 5.1h: Feedback

Topic of today's lesson: the environment

Activities: Feedback

1	We reviewed words from last lesson.	●
2	We read an article about global warming.	● ●
3	We chose five key words and made new sentences.	● ● ●
4	We discussed possible solutions to global warming.	●

Learner self-evaluation

In addition to asking for feedback on your lesson, you may also want to ask your student to evaluate their own input into the lesson (see *Box 5.2a*). This will help the learner to take more responsibility for the lesson and encourage them to reflect on their learning style, preferences and motivation. It will also give you some indirect feedback on your choice of materials and methods. You can also ask for more general reflections on the process of learning one-to-one and see if this changes over time (see *Box 5.2b*).

Box 5.2a: Learner self-evaluation

Name .... Date ....

In today's lesson, I made a lot of progress in ....

....

I put most effort into ....

....

I was most successful at ....

....

I need to work harder on ....

....

From *Learning One-to-One* © Cambridge University Press 2010   PHOTOCOPIABLE

Box 5.2b: Learner self-evaluation

Name .... Date ....

The best thing about learning one-to-one is ....

....

Something that helps me learn is ....

....

Something I've enjoyed in my one-to-one lessons is ....

....

From *Learning One-to-One* © Cambridge University Press 2010   PHOTOCOPIABLE

If you have chosen to use a journal as part of your course design, you can introduce a regular feature of the journal (perhaps once a week or once a month) where students reflect on different aspects of your lessons. An email dialogue or a blog can also be used to obtain ongoing written feedback. Another option is to introduce a learner log. Students can record activities from your lessons, and then say what they learned and reflect on their progress. A learner log can help to develop student self-evaluation skills and independent learning. It can have a variety of formats and is something that you could design in collaboration with your student. *Box 5.3* offers an example.

Box 5.3: Learner log

Date	Activity	What did I learn?	What learning skills did I develop?

From *Learning One-to-One* © Cambridge University Press 2010   PHOTOCOPIABLE

Technology option

If you are teaching online, or by email, it can be very useful to get your student's opinions about the medium of learning as well as the content of the lesson. You can also ask for feedback by email after the lesson (see *Box 5.4* for examples).

Box 5.4: Email feedback

What are the advantages for you of learning online ....
What are the disadvantages? ....

Learning online is better than face-to-face learning because ....
Learning online is not as good as face-to-face learning because ....

Learning online helps me because ....
Learning online is a good way to ....

Summary
- Ask for feedback from your student on a regular basis.
- Be specific about what kind of feedback you want.
- Build up questions gradually to help your student to give useful and constructive feedback.
- Collect different types of written feedback to develop a holistic picture of your student's responses.
- Explain the reasons for collecting feedback.
- Use journals and learner logs to encourage your student to evaluate themselves and their progress.

Recording your reflections on your lessons

> **Reflection**
> *What different methods have you used for reflecting on your lessons? Which ones worked well and why?*

Perhaps the real key to successful one-to-one teaching is developing your ability to reflect on your lessons and to identify what worked, what did not work and why, and by doing so generate your own 'rules' for working with each individual student. This may sound like a laborious process, but I believe that good teachers do this intuitively in a variety of more and less systematic ways.

At the start of your course, you might consider writing a paragraph about what you feel an ideal one-to-one lesson should be like and what your role as a teacher should be. Look back at this later to see if your views have changed, or to see whether you are fulfilling your expectations and if not how you could better achieve this. This kind of reflective writing can also help you explore your key values, which can be especially important when there are cultural differences in student/teacher expectations. (See *Box 5.5* for an example.)

It is useful to keep a record of your own evaluations of lessons. While your student is writing, you can write a couple of sentences about the lesson. Record positive as well as negative reflections because it is easy to become too self-critical and you can often learn as much from what went well as from what did not. *Boxes 5.6a–5.6d* offer some examples of how you might keep records of your observations.

Box 5.5: Teacher journal entry

What do I see as my main role in my one-to-one lessons?

As a one-to-one teacher I want to create a personal friendly atmosphere for learning. It should be quite informal, more like a conversation. I wouldn't like to be talking all the time. I'd like the lessons to be very interactive. I think I should try to encourage my student to speak and ask questions whenever possible. It doesn't matter if I don't know the answers right away. I think I should choose materials carefully so that they are interesting and motivating for my student.

Box 5.6a: Teacher reflection

Date ....
Student ....
Topic ....
Material ....
worked well because ....
....
....
didn't work so well because ....
....
....

From *Learning One-to-One* © Cambridge University Press 2010   PHOTOCOPIABLE

Box 5.6b: Teacher reflection

Date ....
Student ....
Topic ....
Material ....
My general feeling about the lesson ....
....
Things I would do again ....
....
Things I would change ....
....

From *Learning One-to-One* © Cambridge University Press 2010   PHOTOCOPIABLE

Box 5.6c: Teacher reflection

Date ....
Student ....
Topic ....
Material ....
A surprising thing I learned ....

....

A misunderstanding ....

....

From *Learning One-to-One* © Cambridge University Press 2010   PHOTOCOPIABLE

Box 5.6d: Teacher reflection

Date	Student	Topic	What worked well? (Why?)	What didn't work? (Why?)

From *Learning One-to-One* © Cambridge University Press 2010   PHOTOCOPIABLE

The process of taking a few moments to reflect on your lesson will by itself have an impact on your teaching. While you are in the middle of teaching, the opportunities for reflection are limited as you are usually too busy planning what to do next, or thinking about how to respond. So just writing a short comment at the end of the lesson will start a process of reflection that you may not realize until much later.

You can also systematize your reflective process by reviewing your notes and your students' comments and trying to find patterns that will help you design your course more effectively. Could you incorporate a greater variety of learning styles? Could you introduce more opportunities for your learner to take control of the lessons? Evaluating your own and your students' feedback may provide the clues that will help you identify goals for your own professional development.

You may also consider keeping your own teaching journal or blog where you regularly record experiences from your one-to-one lessons. You might set yourself questions such as the following:

- How do I adapt my lessons to suit my students' needs?
- How do I engage my students in the collaborative teaching/learning process?
- How do I make my lessons student-centred?
- How do I help my students develop good study skills and become independent learners?

By answering these questions with specific examples related to specific students and lessons, you can start yourself thinking in more general ways about how to develop teaching skills.

Another way to reflect on your teaching is to record one of your lessons and transcribe a small portion of it. Choose one aspect to analyse – for example the types of questions you ask, or the way you provide feedback. Underline all the examples and see if you can find a pattern. Think of alternative questions or types of feedback that you might have provided in each case. While transcribing the recording can take some time, the type of reflection it can generate can be more transformative as it is based on real rather than remembered data.

Connecting with other one-to-one teachers and sharing experiences and tips is another way to energize your teaching or deal with problems. There are many ESL and ELT blogs online that you can join or read, as well as special-interest group discussion lists for members of organizations like IATEFL or TESOL where you could post questions about one-to-one teaching.

Summary
- Keep a journal or blog to record your perceptions of your role and how it develops.
- Keep a record of your own reflections on each lesson.
- Analyse your records periodically to develop a plan for your professional development.
- Transcribe segments of a lesson and analyse your choices.
- Connect with other one-to-one teachers by joining a blog or online discussion group.

Conclusion

In this chapter, I have described a variety of approaches to obtaining feedback from your learner and to facilitating your own reflection on your teaching. I have argued that getting feedback and reflecting on your teaching are two essential skills for adapting your teaching to the needs of your context. Although asking for feedback may seem a very obvious way of ensuring quality, it is something that teachers often find difficult to do. Sometimes this is because it might seem to put the teacher in a vulnerable position and they might worry about looking insecure. Sometimes it is because it seems unnecessary in a one-to-one context when there is every opportunity for the student to express their concerns. But students may sometimes feel awkward or shy about voicing their opinions and you may only learn about it after they have dropped out. Finding ways to get feedback in a format that is comfortable for you and your student could be the key to successfully engaging your student in the learning process.

Like feedback, reflection is also something that might seem unnecessary and time-consuming. However, particularly in one-to-one teaching where teachers are often working without the support of colleagues, it is important to create a space to dialogue with yourself so that you can see underlying patterns in your teaching style. This enables you to expand on the strategies that work well, and understand how to adapt those that do not. Without systematic reflection, it is tempting to dismiss problems as relating to personality and motivation, when in fact they may be caused by differences in expectations. Reflection ensures continuous engagement with the process of learning, something which is as important for the teacher as it is for the learner.

PART 2 Activities

6 Conversation partner

The activities in this chapter focus on the role of the teacher as conversation partner (see *Chapter 2*, pp. 18–20). Awareness of this role can help you to establish a positive and relaxed learning relationship, building rapport through the exchange of personal information and by exploiting the natural interest generated by talking about genuine experiences and opinions. The activities will help you to fine-tune your teaching to take account of your student's individual needs and language level, and build confidence by encouraging participation and maintaining a sense of progress. There are opportunities to structure and scaffold conversation to enhance learning, and activities can be used as a springboard for grammar- or vocabulary-based work.

6.1 Getting to know you

Outline	You and your student ask each other questions about your favourite things as a way of getting to know each other.
Focus	Talking about personal preferences
Level	Beginner–Intermediate
Time	15–20 minutes
Preparation	Bring two blank cards or create blank boxes on your interactive whiteboard.

Procedure
1 Use the diagram in *Box 6.1* on p. 102 to interview your student, filling in the white areas as shown in the example.
2 Ask your student to interview you and fill out their card.
3 These two cards can go into your student's portfolio if they choose.
4 Use the information to guide you in future lessons on these topics.

Technology option

Work together to create an avatar (online character), choosing their appearance and clothing, and adding a recording of your and your student's voices introducing yourselves and talking about your likes and dislikes. Voki (www.Voki.com), is a useful free online tool that allows you to create personalized speaking avatars and use them on your blog, profile and in email messages.

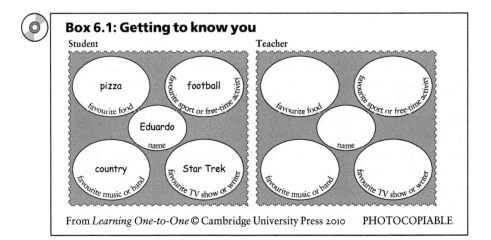

Box 6.1: Getting to know you

From *Learning One-to-One* © Cambridge University Press 2010   PHOTOCOPIABLE

6.2 What do we have in common?

Outline	You and your student exchange personal information as a way of getting to know each other and establishing rapport.
Focus	Talking about likes and dislikes; agreeing and disagreeing
Level	Beginner–Intermediate
Time	20 minutes
Preparation	Make a copy of the Venn diagram in *Box 6.2a* below.

Procedure

1 Explain that the aim of this activity is to make a list of things that you and your student have in common.

2 Explain that you are going to ask each other questions and try to fill out the diagram below with things that you like. In one circle, write the things that you like (but your student does not like), in the other circle write the things that your student likes (but you do not) and in the central overlapping area, write the things that you both like.

3 Take turns asking each other questions in order to find out how many likes you have in common.

4   While talking, model ways of expanding your answers by qualifying them or adding details; and encourage your student to do the same.

5   Keep asking questions until you have ten items in the centre space.

6   When you have reached the target number, summarize your similarities.

7   At this point you may decide to work on some grammar, depending on level, e.g. formation of yes/no questions and wh-questions or 'So do I', or sentences such as *I like tennis and so do you, I like running, but you don't.*

8   To introduce a competitive element, you can award points to the person who successfully elicits the information about a similarity.

9   Keep the diagram for future reference when you want to create language practice examples relevant to your student's interests.

Variations

1   You can use this activity to review other grammar areas such as talking about things you can and cannot do, things you have and have not done, things you want to do and do not want to do in the future.

2   You can use this with other topics such as family, food and diet, free-time activities.

3   Another variation is to try and find similarities between nations (e.g. Japan and Britain are both island nations) or cultural stereotypes. Be mindful, however, of conducting such discussions in a culturally sensitive manner.

4   Instead of a Venn diagram, you can also use a table like the one in *Box 6.2b* on p. 104.

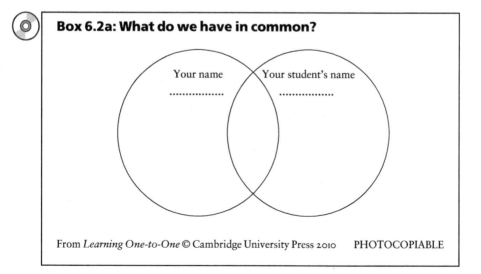

Box 6.2a: What do we have in common?

Your name

....

Your student's name

....

From *Learning One-to-One* © Cambridge University Press 2010   PHOTOCOPIABLE

Box 6.2b: What do we have in common?

		Your student's name	
		Likes	Dislikes
Your name	Likes		
	Dislikes		

This idea is adapted from *Alternatives* by Richard Baudains and Marjorie Baudains, Longman 1990.

6.3 Ask me a question

Outline	You and your student ask each other about personal information.
Focus	Asking wh-questions
Level:	Low intermediate and above
Time	20 minutes
Preparation	Bring a die and a set of cards with a different verb written on each one.

Procedure

1   You and your student take turns to roll the die. Each number on the die corresponds to a different question word as follows: 1 = *what*, 2 = *when*, 3 = *why*, 4 = *who*, 5 = *where*, 6 = *how*.
2   Place the cards face down in the centre of the table. After rolling the die, pick up a card and make a question using the correct question word and the word on the card. For example, if you roll 1 and pick up the word *sing*, you could ask 'What kinds of songs do you sing in the shower?' All the questions should be answered truthfully.

3   If you are able to make a question which can be answered, you get one point. Continue until one person has ten points.

Thank you to Jacqueline French for suggesting this activity.

6.4 Wordpool bingo

Outline	You and your student ask each other questions about personal information to elicit answers from a wordpool.
Focus	Asking questions
Level:	Low intermediate and above
Time	20 minutes
Preparation	Prepare a set of words or phrases you have studied recently, written in the form of a grid.

Procedure

1   Select a pool of words or phrases that you have studied recently. They should be words that can stand alone to form the answers to questions about yourself. Write them on a grid such as the one in *Box 6.4*.

2   You and your student ask questions in order to elicit one of these words or phrases as an answer. For example:

    Question: When do you usually go shopping?
    Answer: At the weekend.
    Question: When do you usually eat cake?
    Answer: On my birthday.

3   If you are successful in making a question and getting an answer, you can cross out the word (using different coloured pens). If you get three in a row (horizontal, vertical or diagonal), you are the winner.

Note

This activity may be best used when you and your student have got to know each other a little, as it involves trying to guess facts about the other person. To extend the conversational aspect of the activity, use one of the questions to lead into a more detailed discussion.

Box 6.4: Wordpool bingo

in January	on my birthday	in December	in the winter	in September
at 10 o'clock	in July	in the evening	on Fridays	at 7 o'clock
on Sunday	on Monday	at night	on Saturday	in July
in the afternoon	in the morning	at the weekend	at lunchtime	at twelve o'clock
in August	in the summer	at 3 pm	in the evening	at 5 o'clock

From *Learning One-to-One* © Cambridge University Press 2010   PHOTOCOPIABLE

Variations
Alternative wordpools:

1   *every day / every week / once a day / once a week / once a month / once a year / often / not very often / sometimes / rarely / never* (Questions: *How often do you . . .? Do you ever . . .?*).
2   *yesterday / last week / a month ago / this morning / next week / tomorrow / in December / next year / in five years* (Questions: *When did you last . . .? When was the last time you . . .? When will you . . .? When do you plan to . . .? When are you going to . . .?*).

6.5 Childhood pictures

Outline	You and your student exchange personal information about your past selves as a way of getting to know each other and establishing rapport.
Focus	Using *used to* for talking about past habits, likes and dislikes
Level	Intermediate and above
Time	20–30 minutes
Preparation	Bring pictures of you when you were younger and ask your student to do the same. Make a copy of the chart in *Box 6.5* below.

Procedure

1   Explain that the activity focuses on describing yourself when you were younger and things about you that have changed.
2   Ask questions about your student's pictures. For example:

How old were you then?

Where/when was it taken?

What were you doing at the time?

Then ask questions about what they used to do and what they used to be like. Review the *used to* form as it comes up in context. Model the questions that you would like your student to ask you later.

3 Fill out a chart about your student.

4 Encourage your student to ask questions about your pictures and questions about what you used to do and be like. Review the *used to* question forms as they come up.

5 Ask your student to fill out a chart about you.

6 Each of you then summarizes the information about the other. Correct any factual errors or add further details.

7 For homework, your student can write a description of how they are different today from in the past.

8 Extension: Ask your student to think of one important event in their life and to consider the effect it had on them. Ask them to describe themselves before and after the event.

Technology option

This activity is one that you could extend by using a collaborative tool like VoiceThread (www.voicethread.com) to create a multimedia slideshow.

Box 6.5: Childhood pictures

	Then	Now
Home		
Job		
Likes/dislikes, e.g. music, sports, TV shows, books, films, food		
Clothing/shoes		
Personality		

From *Learning One-to-One* © Cambridge University Press 2010   PHOTOCOPIABLE

6.6 Your family tree

Outline	You and your student exchange personal information about your families as a way of getting to know each other.
Focus	Using vocabulary to describe family relationships; practising possessive adjectives and possessive *'s*
Level	Intermediate and above
Time	30 minutes
Preparation	Make a copy of one of the diagrams in *Boxes 6.6a–6.6c*.

Procedure

1   Ask your student about their family. As you do so, start drawing a diagram of a family tree with your student at the centre (see examples in *Boxes 6.6a, 6.6b and 6.6c*).

2   Fill in the names of your student's spouse, parents, brothers, sisters, children, etc. Ask for the spellings of names and about their ages, too.

3   As you ask questions, model and draw attention to new words (e.g. pronunciation of 'th' in *brother, mother*), possessive adjectives (*What's her name? What are their names?*) and question forms.

4   Ask your student to check the diagram is correct. Ask them to make sentences about the people in the tree to recycle the vocabulary. For example:

> My brother's name is Carlos.
> His daughter's name is Rosa.

5   Repeat step 1, but this time your student asks you about your family and draws the tree. This stage provides listening practice for your student, so you can challenge them by raising the language level a little or increasing the speed, according to their response.

6   Focus on accuracy in your student's questions, pronunciation and spelling. Check their written work as you go along.

7   Keep the family trees for your next lesson when you can use them to talk about each person's job, where they live, their favourite free-time activities. Add the information to the diagrams and to your student's portfolio.

8   To review the questions and vocabulary again, bring in some photos of your family (ask your students to do the same) and talk about who they are.

Note

It may be best first to ascertain whether your student is comfortable talking about their family. In some cases, for personal or cultural reasons, it may not be a suitable topic for conversation.

Box 6.6a: Your family tree

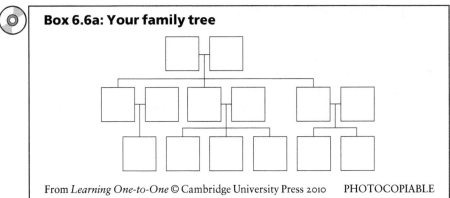

From *Learning One-to-One* © Cambridge University Press 2010   PHOTOCOPIABLE

Box 6.6b: Your family tree

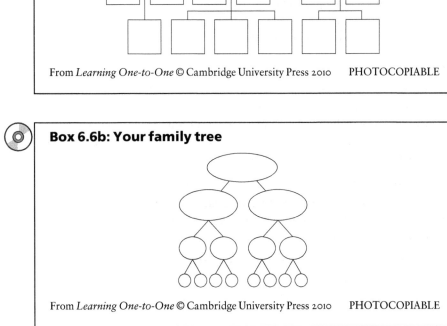

From *Learning One-to-One* © Cambridge University Press 2010   PHOTOCOPIABLE

Box 6.6c: Your family tree

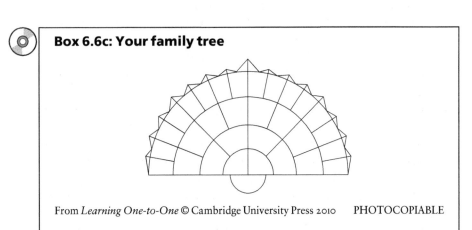

From *Learning One-to-One* © Cambridge University Press 2010   PHOTOCOPIABLE

6.7 Express your feelings

Outline	You and your student exchange personal experiences relating to different emotions as a way of understanding each other's personality and culture.
Focus	Using vocabulary to describe feelings; practising simple present for things that are generally true, and simple past clauses with *when*
Level	Beginner–Intermediate
Time	30 minutes
Preparation	Make a copy of the illustrations in *Box 6.7a* below.

Procedure

1 Review or teach words for feelings shown in the pictures, e.g. *happy, sad, angry, surprised, pleased, upset*, etc.

2 Review the vocabulary by describing a situation for each one. Use intonation and facial expression to give clues. Your student will guess which word describes it best. For example:

> My boyfriend was one hour late for our dinner date! (= *angry*)

(See *Box 6.7b* on p. 112 for other suggestions.)

3 Think of real situations when you experienced these feelings. Start by modelling an example:

> I usually feel upset when someone is late for a meeting. When do you feel upset?

Exchange experiences and find similarities and differences between your experiences.

4 Switch roles. Go back over the pictures, and ask your student to describe the situations and then you guess the emotion, either using their own situations or trying to remember the ones you described.

5 Gradually let your student take over so that they are providing real situations for each word. (You might want to avoid personal topics when talking about negative emotions.)

6 At this point, you can move on to talking about personality (an impatient person gets angry easily, an optimistic person is always happy, etc.). Or you may want to talk about the cultural aspects of some of the situations you have discussed, e.g. whether all people in your culture get upset at lateness, or whether this is a personality issue.

7 Follow up with a homework task: ask your student to choose one situation that you talked about in the lesson and to describe the details. What happened? Where were they? How did they feel? Why did they feel that way? Is this something specific to your student's personality or culture?

Box 6.7a: Express your feelings

Happy

Sad

Angry

Surprised

Annoyed

Pleased

Worried

Upset

Bored

Offended

Fed up

Interested

From *Learning One-to-One* © Cambridge University Press 2010   PHOTOCOPIABLE

Box 6.7b: Express your feelings

My train is one hour late! (= *angry*)
You bought me some chocolates! (= *pleased*)
Oh, I don't have my keys! (= *upset*)
This film is soooo long! (= *bored*)
You are five minutes late. (= *annoyed*)
You locked me out of the office! (= *angry*)
I can't work any more! (= *exhausted*)
It's my birthday and I didn't get any cards. (= *sad*)
My daughter got first place in her class. (= *proud*)
You didn't invite me to your party. (= *offended*)

Note
These emotion cards are also useful for practising and recycling dialogues in role plays. You can choose the cards randomly and role play 'in character' so that the other person can guess which card you have.

6.8 Friends and enemies

Outline	You and your student exchange opinions and personal experiences on the topic of friendship as a way of understanding each other's personality and culture.
Focus	Using vocabulary for describing character and personality; practising relative clauses
Level	Intermediate–Advanced
Time	30 minutes
Preparation	None

Procedure
1 Draw two squares on a piece of paper. One is labelled 'friend' and the other 'enemy'.
2 Explain that you are going to dictate a list of words and your student has to write the words in one of these two boxes.
3 Start by dictating some fairly easy words, e.g. *kind, loyal, dishonest, lie, help*.
4 Continue with some more ambiguous words, e.g. *strong, sad, problem, talk, argue*.

5 Now ask your student about the words. Why did they choose to put them in those boxes? Respond with your own feelings and opinions about these words and compare similarities or differences.
6 Ask your student to add more words to each box.
7 Use the words in each box to make definitions of a friend or an enemy. For example:

> A friend is someone who is kind, loyal, and never lies to you.
> An enemy is someone who cheats and betrays you, and causes problems in your life.

Variations
Other topics: happiness and sadness, love and hate, tolerance and intolerance, a good or bad manager, a good or bad employee, an interesting or a boring job.

Technology option
One idea for extending this activity into more creative writing is to create a poem based on the words in the boxes. It can be fun to go to a website that uses the idea of magnetic poetry (words on magnets that can be moved around on a board), for example Magnetic Poetry® (www.magneticpoetry.com/educat.html), which has some free online tools for doing this.

6.9 How green are you?

Outline	You and your student compare strategies for recycling, to find similarities and differences in your lifestyles.
Focus	Using vocabulary for talking about environmental issues; practising modals such as *should, ought to, have to, would like to*
Level	Intermediate–Advanced
Time	30 minutes
Preparation	Make a copy of the questionnaire in *Box 6.9* on p.114.

Procedure
There are various ways of using this material. Here are some suggestions:
1 Ask your student to interview you using the questions in *Box 6.9,* and find out which ones you do, your student does, and that you both do.

Box 6.9: How green are you?

Which of these do you do?	You	Your teacher
At home		
1 Recycle metal, glass, plastic and paper		
2 Buy energy-efficient appliances		
3 Reuse plastic bags at the supermarket		
4 Turn off lights and appliances at night		
5 Hang up your laundry to dry		
6		
7		
8		
At work		
1 Recycle paper, plastic and glass		
2 Buy recycled paper		
3 Make two-sided copies		
4 Take the bus, walk or ride your bike to work		
5 Use teleconferencing instead of driving to meetings		
6 Work at home one or more days a week		
7		
8		
In your car		
1 Join a neighbourhood carpool for shopping		
2 Recycle oil, batteries and tyres		
3 Have your car's emissions tested regularly		
4 Remove unnecessary items from your car		
5 Check tyre pressure regularly		
6 Avoid accelerating rapidly		
7		
8		

2   As you do so, exchange reasons as to why you do or do not do these things. Identify those that you would like to do and those that you would never do.
3   Choose the top ten suggestions that are most practical and that most people in your community are likely to do right now.
4   Categorize the topics into those that are about recycling, saving energy, preventing pollution or all three. Perhaps you will find some that do not really help the environment.
5   Add more suggestions to each category.
6   Choose the top three and write a letter to your boss recommending these changes.
7   Create a poster to persuade your neighbours to implement the top five suggestions.

Variations
1   This topic could be adapted to your student's occupation and a discussion of the environmental impact of work and production practices in their company.
2   This activity could be adapted to other topics such as health (how healthy is your lifestyle?), technology (how tech-savvy are you?) and work (how hardworking/enterprising/conscientious are you?).

6.10 Guess what I have

Outline	You and your student find out about each other through objects that you carry with you every day.
Focus	Practising yes/no and wh-questions
Level	High beginner and above
Time	20 minutes
Preparation	None

Procedure
1   Think of an object that you have with you today in your bag or pocket, or something you are wearing.
2   Invite your student to ask yes/no questions to try and find out what it is.
3   When they have guessed correctly, encourage them to use wh-questions to discover the story behind the object. As you tell the story, encourage your student to exchange similar experiences.
4   Switch roles. This time you must try to guess an object that the student has / is wearing.

Variations

1   Use an object that has a special meaning for you or your student, e.g. a lucky charm or a souvenir.
2   For homework, ask your student to write a description of the object and the story behind it.

6.11 Holiday postcards

Outline	You and your student exchange experiences and recommendations about places to go on holiday.
Focus	Practising holiday vocabulary; writing a postcard message
Level	Elementary–Intermediate
Time	20–30 minutes
Preparation	Bring in a holiday brochure or a collection of pictures of different places suitable for a holiday.

Procedure

1   Look at your selection of pictures together. Ask your student to choose two pictures of places they would love to visit and two places they would hate. Do the same yourself.
2   Ask each other questions to find out which pictures are which, e.g. *Do you love warm tropical places?*
3   Discuss what these pictures tell about your personalities and the types of holidays you enjoy. Use this opportunity to exchange tips and experiences of good and bad holidays.
4   Interview your student about an imaginary holiday in this place. For example:

> Where are you?
> What are you doing?
> What is the weather like?
> What is the food like?

As you do so, build up a set of vocabulary under different headings (food, weather, leisure activities).
5   Switch roles and ask your student to interview you about one of your pictures.

6 Brainstorm the types of topics that people usually write about when sending a postcard on holiday, e.g. weather, food, sightseeing, leisure activities.

7 Study an example of a postcard message (your own, or use the example in *Box 6.11* below). Notice the stylistic features (omission of subject pronouns and auxiliaries), the greeting and the closing.

8 Help your student to write a postcard message that is appropriate for their picture.

9 Ask them to send you a postcard for homework.

Notes

This activity allows students to have some control over the content of the lesson according to their preferences. You can facilitate by helping them find the words to describe their real experiences.

Technology option

Ask your student to send you an e-postcard. Suggest that they visit the website www.postcards.org and choose categories 'nature and outdoors' or 'landmarks' for some scenic pictures. You can also download free postcard templates online.

Box 6.11: Holiday postcards

Hi Judy,

Having a lot of fun here in Greece. The weather is wonderful and the sea is really warm. We go swimming and diving every day. I love Greek food! Hope you're having a good holiday. See you soon.
Love, Kristin

....
....
....
....

6.12 The power of advertising

Outline	You and your student compare your reactions to advertisements, to talk about how people respond to advertising.
Focus	Using vocabulary for describing pictures, feelings, moods; practising structures such as: *it makes you think of . . ., it persuades you to . . ., it gives the impression that . . .*
Level	Intermediate–Advanced
Time	30 minutes
Preparation	Bring in a selection of 3–5 magazine/newspaper ads in English or a video of ads from TV or YouTube™.

Procedure

1 Discuss some different ways of advertising in print and online media. Exchange opinions about whether advertising is good, bad or just annoying.

2 Explain that you are going to look at some ads together and decide what kinds of methods they use. For example, some might use a famous person, or humour, or a pun on words (see *Box 6.12*).

3 After looking at the ads, put them away, and give your student two minutes to write down all the ads they can remember, or the most memorable points of any of the ads.

4 You do the same. Then compare your lists.

5 Discuss why some of the ads were more memorable than others and try to explain the reasons for any differences in your lists. What was similar and different about your lists?

6 Talk about any other ads that either of you has seen recently and why you liked/disliked them and why they are memorable.

7 Follow up with a reading about advertising techniques for homework.

Box 6.12: The power of advertising

	Advertisement 1	
1	Type of product	
2	Brand name	
3	Advertising technique	
4	Memorable words or image	
5	Like / dislike / no opinion	

From *Learning One-to-One* © Cambridge University Press 2010   PHOTOCOPIABLE

6.13 Work pie

Outline	You and your student exchange information about your typical work day by describing work activities and categorizing them.
Focus	Using vocabulary for describing work activities; practising the simple present for everyday routines and adverbs of frequency
Level	Intermediate–Advanced
Time	20 minutes
Preparation	None

Procedure

1   Ask your student to list out their typical workday activities.
2   Try to find ways of grouping them so that they can be divided into different categories, e.g. talking on the phone, answering emails, writing letters, reading contracts, negotiating.
3   Ask your student to estimate how much of the work day is spent on each activity.
4   Create a pie chart based on this information (see *Box 6.13* on p. 120 for an example).
5   Discuss which sections of the pie your student would like to spend more or less time on.

6   List out some suggestions for doing this. For example, if your student feels they spend too much time checking and sending emails, you might think of ways to reduce this, e.g. by flagging important emails in order of priority, only checking emails twice a day, etc.

7   Switch roles. Ask your student to guess what your workday pie is like. They should try to draw and fill out the pie based on the information they get from you. Invite them to ask you similar questions about which sections of the pie you would like to spend less/more time on and how to achieve this.

8   Round up this activity with an action plan on how to improve your working day and make your work time more effective.

Variation
Instead of work, talk about free-time or weekend activities.

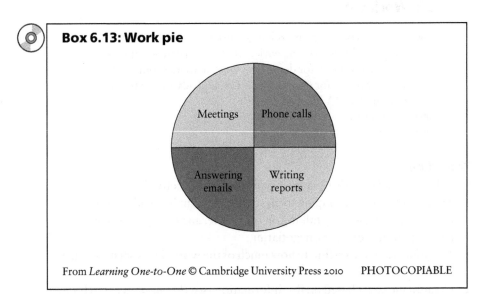

Box 6.13: Work pie

From *Learning One-to-One* © Cambridge University Press 2010   PHOTOCOPIABLE

This idea is adapted from *Lessons from the Learner: Student-Generated Activities for the Language Classroom* by Sheelagh Deller, Longman 1990.

6.14 Well done!

Outline	You and your student talk about your personal achievements.
Focus	Using vocabulary to describe personal achievements positively (e.g. verbs such as *introduced, implemented, created, developed, designed*); practising ways of showing appreciation for others
Level	Intermediate–Advanced
Time	30 minutes
Preparation	None

Procedure

1　Brainstorm any achievements your student is particularly proud of at work. These might date back to when they first started their job, or they might have occurred during the last year, or even the last week. Give some examples, such as improving a system for maintaining quality assurance, or introducing paper recycling into their workplace. Give other examples from your own experience and compare them.

2　Role play telling a colleague about this achievement. Practise ways of responding to this. For example:

> Well done!
> Good work!
> What a great idea!
> That sounds very practical/useful/efficient/interesting/innovative.

3　Go through the list, switching roles as you do so (so that sometimes you are playing the role of your student).

4　Discuss how comfortable/acceptable this kind of conversation would be in their workplace and why they would or would not ever do this. This may develop into a cultural comparison (see *Note* below).

5　Turn the dialogue into an email to a colleague thanking or praising them for their work (see *Box 6.14* on p. 122).

Note

It may be interesting to discuss cultural differences relating to talking about one's own achievements. In some cultures it is considered immodest to show off, while in others it is considered a sign of confidence.

Box 6.14: Well done!

From: Rachel
To: Annabel
Subject: New sign on coffee machine

Hi Annabel:

I noticed that you recently put up a new sign near the coffee machine to remind us to recycle our paper cups or use our own cups to save paper. What a good idea! It's very useful to be reminded of ways to save the environment. Thank you.

Rachel

---

7 Observer and listener

The activities in this chapter focus on the role of the teacher as observer and listener (see *Chapter 2*, pp. 21–5). Awareness of this role enables you to carefully observe your student's responses in order to find out what they need to learn (what are the gaps in their linguistic knowledge?) and how best to help them learn it (what learning styles suit them best?). In many of these activities, the teacher can take a back seat, allowing the learner the space to direct the interaction. This gives you, as the observer, the chance to look and listen for clues in their levels of interest and motivation that can help you to plan future lessons. You may decide to take notes of some of your observations as suggested in *Chapter 2*.

7.1 Ask the right question

Outline	You provide answers to questions about yourself, and your student tries to guess the question, giving you the opportunity to notice which kinds of questions are difficult for them.
Focus	Talking about personal information; asking questions
Level	Any
Time	15–20 minutes
Preparation	None

Procedure
1   Write down the answers to some personal questions about yourself. Do not say or write the questions. (You can write the answers one at a time, or write a group of five or six answers to start off with and ask your student to select the ones they want to try first.)
2   Your student will try to work out what the questions are.
3   Start with easy ones, and gradually make them more difficult. Continue until you find one that your student really struggles with and focus on this as your grammar point of the lesson.

4   To increase the challenge, introduce some answers that could have more than one possible question. For example:

Teacher writes:	Sarah.	Student asks:	What's your name?
Teacher writes:	670-5566.	Student asks:	What's your phone number?
Teacher writes:	Twenty-eight.	Student asks:	How old are you?
Teacher writes:	London.	Student asks:	Where were you born?
Teacher writes:	Swimming.	Student asks:	What's your favourite sport? / What kind of sport do you like? / What sport do you like best?

5   At the end, switch roles or review all the questions again, this time focusing on fluency and intonation, or ask your student to write them out for homework in order to focus on accuracy.

7.2 Grammar auction

Outline	Your student analyses sentences from their homework and tries to identify which ones are correct, giving you the opportunity to notice which grammar points are difficult for them.
Focus	Any
Level	Any
Time	20–30 minutes
Preparation	Make a list of ten sentences from your student's oral or written work, five with mistakes, and five without; bring in around 20 plastic markers (like tiddlywinks), or small plastic dots, or coloured sticky dots.

Procedure

1   Explain that you are going to work on some common grammar mistakes. Give your student the list you have prepared (you can choose them from your student's homework, or write them down quickly during a speaking exercise). About half of them should contain one clearly identifiable mistake.

2 Explain the rules of a 'grammar auction': They can use their 'money' (the plastic dots) to 'buy' sentences that they think are correct. If they are right, they will double their money. If they are wrong, they will lose the money they bet. (You may want to set a target total amount if they want to 'win'.)

3 Allow some quiet time for your student to read and think about the sentences, and place the dots according to how confident they are about the accuracy of the sentences.

4 When bets are final, go through all the ones with bets and calculate the winnings.

5 Correct the incorrect sentences together. Ask your student to write the corrections.

6 Use this as a springboard to discuss the reasons for some common mistakes.

Note

It is useful to make an extra copy of the sentences for yourself. While your student is going through the sentences, you can observe and note which ones they found easy, and which ones they had difficulty with and why.

Variations

1 Prepare a list of incorrect sentences and ask your student to bet on the ones they are sure they can correct.

2 Prepare a list of incorrect sentences that all have the same type of mistake (e.g. articles or prepositions) and use it to lead into a review of this grammar point.

3 Prepare sentences with vocabulary errors such as those with cognates and false friends (some correct and some incorrect).

Note

This activity provides a good opportunity for students to ask grammar questions that really interest them and to use metalanguage to discuss common grammar problems. It is also very positive if they can successfully explain why a sentence is wrong and provide the correct answer. To introduce an element of competition, you can keep a record of their score each time so they can try to beat their previous record.

This idea is adapted from *Grammar Games* by Mario Rinvolucri, Cambridge University Press 1984.

7.3 What's the word I need?

Outline	Your student speaks about a topic of their choice, asking you for vocabulary as needed.
Focus	Any
Level	Any
Time	20–30 minutes
Preparation	None

Procedure

1 Invite your student to choose a topic to talk about.
2 Encourage them to speak as much as possible and avoid interrupting or prompting.
3 Every time they are stuck for a word, give them the word and ask them to write it down.
4 Keep a running list of the vocabulary and go over it at the start of the next lesson.

This idea is based on a technique used in Counseling-Learning, developed in *Counseling-Learning in Second Languages* by Charles A. Curran, Apple River Press 1976.

7.4 Verb cards

Outline	Your student uses verb cards to talk about past events, giving you the opportunity to notice which verb forms are difficult for them.
Focus	Practising past tense forms
Level	Any
Time	20 minutes
Preparation	Bring in about 16–20 small squares of blank paper or card.

Procedure

1 Warm up with a brief chat about what your student did yesterday, last weekend or last vacation. Do not correct anything, but make a note of any past tense verbs that come up.
2 Write one verb (base / bare infinitive form) on each square. Start off by suggesting a few verbs yourself, gradually letting your student take over.
3 Spread the papers out on the table. Ask your student to choose one and say the past form. Every time they remember a verb successfully, they can pick up the card and put it in a separate pile. (*Note:* Don't give any hints until the very end when there might be some verbs that they really can't

remember. Then, if possible, think of some useful hint or mnemonic to help them.)

4   Shuffle the papers and put them in a pile. Ask your student to divide them into two piles: things they did yesterday and things they did not do, making a true sentence each time. For example, for the verb *go*, either *I went to the library* or *I didn't go anywhere*. You can repeat this stage by asking again about last weekend or about their last vacation or trip. Each time they make a correct sentence, the student should pick up the paper and put it into the appropriate pile.

5   Shuffle the papers again and lay them out as in stage 3. This time, your student asks you questions in the past using the verbs. You'll get a variety of wh- and yes/no questions, depending on the verbs that have been selected. (*Note:* As before, your student can choose the sequence, probably choosing the ones they feel most confident about first. Only allow your student to 'take' the card when they have produced a correct sentence. Do not provide any prompts until the end.)

6   Give true answers to your student's questions. Then ask your student to describe what you did yesterday.

7   As a final stage, ask your student to make sentences for each verb, starting with 'I' and finishing in as many different ways as possible. For example:

> I walked . . . to the library, on the beach, in the garden, etc.
> I had . . . a shower, chicken for dinner, a good time, etc.

You may want to write these on the backs of the cards for review next time.

Variations

1   Use different coloured pens to differentiate past forms from base forms, or regular from irregular verbs, or verbs from other parts of the sentence.

2   This activity could be adapted to other tenses and modals, e.g. things they might do or will do; things they can do or cannot do; things they have done already, things they have not done yet.

Notes

The advantages of this activity are that the student can choose the sequence they feel most comfortable with and can work at their own speed. Picking up and moving the cards around gives a feeling of ownership and progress and engages the kinesthetic learning mode. As an observer, you can make note of the verbs your student finds most difficult and review them more frequently next time.

7.5 Specialist vocabulary

Outline	Your student describes their day at work in detail, giving you the opportunity to identify vocabulary related to their job or specialization.
Focus	Expanding specialized vocabulary
Level	Any
Time	20 minutes
Preparation	Prepare a chart such as the one in *Box 7.5*.

Procedure

1 Ask your student to talk about their day at work yesterday, or last week. Get them to describe it in as much detail as possible. What tasks did they do? Who did they talk to? What tools and equipment did they use?

2 As you listen, take notes of the vocabulary used by your student under these headings (see *Box 7.5*). The aim is to build up a vocabulary bank of some of the specialist vocabulary related to your student's occupation.

3 Evaluate the words in the list together and decide if they are being used accurately. Add extra related words or subcategories to refine the list. Cross out words that are not specific enough and replace them. Use the dictionary to verify specialized meanings.

4 Choose one word or set of words in the chart to elaborate into a mind map of related words and collocations.

5 Use the chart to create future quizzes and puzzles for your student to help them remember the words.

Technology option

You can easily create crosswords and other word puzzles using free online tools such as the following: www.puzzlemaker.discoveryeducation.com and www.edhelper.com/puzzles.htm. The puzzles can be printed out, or stored online.

Box 7.5: Specialist vocabulary			
Job titles	**Tools/Equipment**	**Places/Buildings**	**Activities/Tasks**

From *Learning One-to-One* © Cambridge University Press 2010   PHOTOCOPIABLE

7.6 Tell me my story

Outline	Your student chooses an interesting anecdote to tell about themselves, helping you to identify specific language that they need. Then you retell the story back to them.
Focus	Practising fluency and use of idiomatic language
Level	Intermediate–Advanced
Time	30 minutes
Preparation	None

Procedure

1 Invite your student to think of a story or anecdote to tell you. For example:

- the funniest (or most embarrassing, frightening) thing that ever happened to me
- a strange coincidence
- a misunderstanding
- doing someone a favour.

2 Listen carefully and when they have finished, tell the story back to your student, using correct English, and introducing helpful and interesting vocabulary and idioms as appropriate.

3 Your student then retells the story using target forms and new vocabulary.

4 Repeat stages 2 and 3 as many times as necessary.

Note

While you are listening, try to picture their experience and the kinds of words and language that will help them express their ideas better.

This idea is adapted from *Success with Foreign Languages* by Earl Stevick, Prentice Hall 1989.

7.7 Your earliest memory

Outline	Your student chooses an early childhood memory to talk about. You listen and fill out the chart. This gives you the opportunity to identify clues to their learning style.
Focus	Practising descriptive vocabulary
Level	Intermediate–Advanced
Time	30 minutes
Preparation	Make a copy of the chart in *Box 7.7*.

Procedure

1 Ask your student to close their eyes and think of their earliest, or a very early, memory.

2 As your student describes the memory to you, make notes of key words or expressions under the headings in the chart. For example, if your student describes a scene full of colours and shapes, these words may go under 'visual', or if they use words like *the sound of . . .* or *it sounds like . . .*, it may go under 'auditory'.

3 Go over the chart with your student to see if they agree with the headings you have chosen. Any disagreements will generate a good discussion of more specific details.

4 Reverse roles and ask your student to fill out a chart as you describe your first memory.

5 Evaluate the two charts together to decide which of you is the more visual, auditory or kinesthetic, or has a stronger sense of smell or taste.

6 Depending on the senses that your student seems to use more, try adding some new words to their chart. For example, you might add words for describing their memory in visual terms (*bright, blurred, hazy*), auditory terms (*loud, quiet, shouting, whispering*), or ways of moving (*crawling, spinning, racing*).

7 Ask your student to retell the memory, using the new expressions. Alternatively, try retelling the memory using all the different senses.

Variations

Other topics for this activity might be: your first date, your first English (or foreign language) lesson, your first job, the best meal you have ever had, the most unusual food you have ever eaten, the most unusual sport you have ever tried.

Box 7.7: Your earliest memory

Visual	Auditory	Kinesthetic	Smell	Taste

From *Learning One-to-One* © Cambridge University Press 2010   PHOTOCOPIABLE

This activity was inspired by a workshop given by Bonnie Tsai at the IATEFL conference in Cardiff in 2009 called 'NLP: It's not what you think'. (*Note:* This type of chart is used frequently in Neuro-Linguistic Programming (NLP).)

7.8 Describe this room

Outline	Your student moves around the room and describes objects, giving you the opportunity to identify their grammar and vocabulary needs as well as noticing clues to their learning style.
Focus	Practising vocabulary for everyday objects, and prepositions of location
Level	Beginner and above
Time	15–20 minutes
Preparation	None

Procedure

1 Ask your student to walk around the room and say the name of every object they know the word for (e.g. *chair, table, picture, poster, light, cup, glass, computer, door, wall, window*, etc.). If they run out, prompt them by pointing.

2 Present or review simple prepositions of location (*in, on, next to, in front of, above, under, behind, between*), illustrating the meaning with examples of objects around the room.

3 Ask questions with *where* using both singular and plural nouns. For example:

> Where is the clock?
> Where are the pencils?

4 Ask your student to answer with sentences using the correct preposition. Then switch roles. Each time, invite them to go and touch or point to the object they are asking about or describing.

> Teacher: Where is the cup?
> Student: It's on the table. Where are the pencils?
> Teacher: They're in the cup.

5 Repeat step 4, but one of you closes your eyes and the other asks the questions. Switch roles.

6 Ask your student to close their eyes (or step outside the room for a moment). Move one object (or more) to a new location. When your student returns, they will identify the new location of the object. Switch roles.

7 Ask questions with *How many . . .?* For example:

> How many books are there on the shelf?

Repeat steps 4 and 5.

8 You may expand the activity to describe the building you are in (*How many offices are there on the first floor?*), or to describe their home (*How many rooms are there in your home?*).

Note

While doing this activity, you can observe whether your student responds well to a kinesthetic learning style. You may also come across other grammar points that need work, e.g. articles, plurals, count and non-count nouns, and these may be used as a basis for the next lesson.

7.9 Choosing categories

Outline	Your student compares different jobs in order to define what factors are most important to them when choosing a job.
Focus	Practising vocabulary to describe jobs, job duties and characteristics of jobs
Level	Intermediate and above
Time	20–30 minutes
Preparation	Bring in a set of blank cards / squares of paper and a selection of job ads (from the newspaper or the internet) of various different types of job, e.g. driver, gardener, chef, daycare, nursing, administrative assistant. Or bring in pictures of jobs, or write names of jobs on separate cards.

Procedure

1 Explain that the purpose of the lesson is to discuss what factors are most important when choosing a job.

2 Skim the job ads and check that your student understands the type of job in each ad.

3 Invite your student to choose three of the jobs and say which they would most like to do.

4 Ask your student to choose two of these three jobs and explain how they are different from the third.

5 Your student then gives a reason for preferring two of the jobs as opposed to the third (or one as opposed to the two others) in terms of a value judgement. For example:

> I'd prefer to be a driver or a gardener because you can organize your own schedule, but a chef is told what to do and when to do it by someone else.

6 Write on a card a short summary of the student's criterion, e.g. 'freedom to organize schedule'. Check that the student agrees that this is the value that they expressed, and put the card aside. This value judgement will form the first in a list of 'constructs' that they can later use to evaluate their own job, or a new job that they want to apply for. (*Note:* The essential element here is that all constructs come from the student and are not prompted by the teacher.)

7 Put the selected job or jobs to one side and continue with groups of three from the other jobs. Summarize the student's criterion on a card, as before, and add it to the criterion cards.

8 Continue until only one job remains.

9 At the end, ask the learner to choose any job that they would really like to do. Take the pile of criterion cards, and ask the student to rate their ideal job against their own criteria.

Variations
Instead of focusing on jobs, try countries they would like to visit, sports they would like to try, books or films they have read/seen, relationships at work, experiences of learning.

This idea is adapted from a research interviewing technique called Personal Construct Theory, developed by George Kelly. For more information, see: www.enquirewithin.co.nz/HINTS/skills2.htm.

7.10 Picture dictation

Outline	Your student describes their work space and you draw a picture of it. Then you discuss how it could be improved.
Focus	Practising vocabulary needed to describe your student's work space, prepositions of location, adjectives with *too* and *not . . . enough,* and comparative forms
Level	Intermediate and above
Time	20–30 minutes
Preparation	None

Procedure

1 Start by asking your student to describe their work space to you. As you listen, draw a diagram of their work space.

2 Supply new vocabulary as needed, and ask your student to keep a list of all the new words.

3 Ask your student what is good and bad about their workplace. Discuss some suggestions for improving it.

4 While you are doing this, notice whether your student is using structures such as *too* and *not . . . enough* with adjectives (e.g. *It's too hot. It isn't quiet enough. There isn't enough light*). If so, you may use this as a springboard to teaching more adjectives and using a short drill to practise this grammar point.

5 Switch roles and dictate a picture of your previous workplace to your student. Invite them to ask you questions about ways to improve it, too.

6 Ask them to compare two workplaces, perhaps one from their previous job and their current job. This provides an opportunity to notice their use of comparisons. Are they using comparisons with short and long adjectives correctly? Are they using the structure *not as . . . as* or comparisons with qualifiers such as *far smaller than, much nicer than, not quite as . . . as, not nearly as . . . as,* etc.

7 If you are online, find pictures of work spaces and describe what is good or bad about them (use Google Image Search™).

8 Develop a set of guidelines for managers/companies on priorities for creating suitable work spaces for their employees. Or develop a questionnaire to find out what employees think about their work space. (The student may be able to interview someone at work about this for homework and present the results in your next lesson.)

Variations

Ask your student to describe a different space, e.g. their living room, kitchen or study space. Or ask them to draw a map of their neighbourhood and to say how they think the neighbourhood could be improved.

Technology option

A picture dictation is a fun way to use a collaborative editing tool like Twiddla (www.twiddla.com).

7.11 Rules and regulations

Outline	Your student describes rules in a context familiar to them, giving you the opportunity to notice which modals they have difficulty with.
Focus	Practising modal verbs, e.g. *have to, don't have to, must, can, are allowed to, are not allowed to*
Level	Beginner–Advanced
Time	20–30 minutes
Preparation	None

Procedure

1 Start off by talking about a context in your student's experience where there are rules and regulations, e.g. their workplace, driving a car, going to the gym or the pool.

2 While you are talking, supply any useful vocabulary but do not correct any grammar.

3 Notice which modal verbs your student is using, whether they are being used correctly and which ones are not being used.

4 Start making a list (based on which rules have come up in your conversation) of different endings for sentences with modal verbs. For example, if the topic was driving, your list might be as follows:

> . . . stop at a red light
> . . . drive on the right
> . . . wear a seatbelt in the front
> . . . wear a seatbelt in the back
> . . . have a driving license
> . . . wear a helmet
> . . . smoke

     . . . drink alcohol
     . . . use a cellphone
     . . . listen to the radio.

5   Introduce the modal verbs that you want to teach and use your list to practise a short drill on each of the verbs.

6   Turn each one into a question. For example:

     Do you have to wear a seatbelt?
     Are you allowed to use a cellphone?

7   Talk about differences in these rules between different countries.

8   Transfer to another situation, e.g. the workplace (. . . wear a suit and tie, . . . make personal phone calls, etc.)

9   Describe some rules that you agree with and some that you do not agree with and say why. Write about this for homework.

7.12 The grab bag

Outline	Your student chooses an object from a bag of objects and talks about it for two minutes, giving you the opportunity to identify their language needs.
Focus	Practising vocabulary for colours, shapes, smells, textures, fabrics; practising structures such as: *It looks like something for . . . It's similar to . . . It might be something people use to . . . It reminds me of . . . It makes me think of . . . It's good/useful/interesting/dangerous because . . . It's made of/from . . .*
Level	Beginner–Advanced
Time	10–15 minutes
Preparation	Bring in about six objects that suggest imaginative stories (see *Ideas* below). They can be simple everyday objects (e.g. a teaspoon, a comb, a key) and could also include one or two unusual or personal objects (e.g. a photograph, a ring). They should be small enough to collect in a small paper bag. Put the objects into a paper bag (do not show them to your student).

Procedure

1   Ask your student to close their eyes, put their hand in the bag and choose one object. Their task is to talk about it for two minutes without pausing or interruption from the teacher.

2 You may find it helpful to provide a starting sentence, such as, 'Today I'm going to talk about this (name of object). This object is very interesting because . . .'

3 After two minutes are up, you may continue by asking further questions about the object.

Ideas for groups of objects

- Food: an egg, a packet of biscuits, a yogurt, a teabag, a package of sugar, pepper, salt or coffee
- Environment: contrasting objects made of plastic, paper, glass, nylon, polyester, cotton, wool, etc.
- Hobbies: objects representing a variety of hobbies, e.g. a toy car, a cooking utensil, a table-tennis ball, a stamp)
- Holidays: objects relevant to local customs or typical holiday celebrations, e.g. Christmas (an Xmas cracker, a tree decoration, a piece of holly)
- Different types of text: piece of a newspaper headline, piece of an email, concert or cinema ticket, bus or train ticket, envelope with address, food package label.

Variations

1 Instead of talking for two minutes, invite your student to ask as many questions as possible about the object. At the end of the time limit, see how many questions you can answer together. Use one of the questions as a starter for a journal entry or written homework assignment.

2 Ask your student to make up a story about the object, imagining where it came from, who made it, how it was made, who has used it and what happened to it. This can later be used as the basis for a free writing exercise in their journal or a written homework assignment.

3 Instead of using objects, try photographs or pictures from magazines.

Notes

This activity will enable you to learn a great deal about your student without asking lots of questions. You may, for example, observe that their learning style responds well to the visual/tactile element of this game and decide to incorporate similar elements in other lessons.

Feedback provider

The activities in this chapter focus on the role of the teacher as feedback provider (see *Chapter 2*, pp. 25–31). Awareness of this role will help you to think about how and when to give feedback to your student and what kind of feedback to provide. The activities entail using some of the feedback techniques mentioned in *Chapter 2* and suggest separating different stages of feedback, for example feedback on meaning from feedback on form. They also suggest ways of encouraging your student to participate in the feedback process by developing their own self-evaluative criteria so that they can become more independent learners.

8.1 Correcting written homework

Outline	Your student reads their homework aloud, and you provide feedback to help them identify and correct errors.
Focus	Practising editing skills and checking for accuracy in written work
Level	Any
Time	15–20 minutes
Preparation	None

Procedure

1 Ask your student to write a short paragraph for homework.
2 In the next lesson, read through your student's homework silently, mentally noting the errors you would like to correct, but without making any marks on the page.
3 Give some positive feedback on the overall content, organization or vocabulary. Then explain that you are going to focus on grammatical accuracy.
4 Ask your student to read the paragraph aloud to you. Stop them when there is an error. For example:

Your student has written:
I have one son. My son six years old. He goes elementary school.
Your student reads aloud:
I have one son. My son . . . (You indicate that there is an error here by using a gesture, repeating the part before the error (*'My son . . .?'*) and pausing as if for a missing word, or mouthing the word silently.)

5 Help your student to correct the errors in their own handwriting.

6 Finally, ask your student to read the paragraph again without mistakes.

Variations

1 Reading aloud sometimes encourages stilted intonation, so you could also use this activity to contrast slow, careful enunciation of each word with a more fluent and rhythmical intonation flow. You could also contrast full forms and contracted forms, or focus on specific pronunciation problems.

2 To improve writing skills, you could ask questions about each part of the paragraph to help students see how to expand their ideas by incorporating more information and how to create complex sentences by adding subordinate clauses.

3 You could also focus on sentence-to-sentence cohesion at this stage: is it clear how each sentence within a paragraph is connected to the previous one through the use of cohesive devices such as referring expressions, conjunctions, word repetition or synonyms?

Note

The advantage of this type of feedback is that your student ends up with a correct version in their own handwriting and they can ask questions about the errors. Reading aloud is also a useful strategy for students to check their own work.

8.2 Transcribing a one-minute talk

Outline	You record a short talk by your student and your student transcribes the talk for homework. In the next lesson, you go over the transcription together and make any corrections or improvements before recording the talk again.
Focus	Any
Level	Any
Time	20–30 minutes
Preparation	Bring in a portable recording device to your lesson.

Procedure

1 Ask your student to choose a topic for a one-minute talk. It could be something you have talked about recently, or something new related to their job or study. Here are some suggestions (increasing in level of difficulty):

- My first day at school
- Something I lost
- The time I won something
- My worst hair experience
- Experience is the best teacher
- Why I work
- If there were 25 hours in the day
- My desert island book
- How technology changed my life
- The neighbours from hell
- My dream vacation
- An animal encounter
- The most famous person I never met (but would like to)
- The best advice I was ever given
- How I shop for food.

2 Record your student's one-minute talk. Do not interrupt or correct.

3 Give feedback on the general content (what was most interesting or surprising?). Ask questions or continue the discussion at the end if appropriate.

4 For homework, your student can transcribe their talk and bring the transcript to the next lesson (if the whole recording is too long, they can choose just one small part).

5 Go over the transcript together (see *Chapter 2*, pp. 29–30 on feedback techniques for written work). Work on grammar, vocabulary, and then add or clarify information.

6 Ask your student to make corrections and improvements on the page as you go through it. Then record the talk again.

7 The transcript and the recording can go into their portfolio.

Variations

1 For business English and ESP, ask your student to choose a topic specifically related to their field, or ask them to explain a key concept in their area of specialization.

2 Instead of a one-minute talk, ask your student to record a conversation with you and transcribe one section of it at home. Go over the transcript together. Then redo the role play together.

This idea is adapted from *Doing Task-Based Teaching* by Dave Willis and Jane Willis, Oxford University Press 2007.

8.3 Improving your résumé

Outline	Your student evaluates some sample résumés and then works on improving their own résumé, giving you the opportunity to provide feedback on layout, organization, content, style and accuracy.
Focus	Practising writing skills
Level	Intermediate–Advanced
Time	40–60 minutes, could be spread over several lessons
Preparation	Bring in some sample résumés/CVs, or send your student links to sample résumés/CVs online. Some websites providing samples and tips may be found in the *Websites* section on pp. 202–3.

Procedure

1   Look at the sample résumés you have brought or found online.

2   Provide some questions to help your student evaluate the résumés. Use the questions to generate a list of criteria for improving a résumé. These criteria will depend on the type of job, but some general questions are suggested in *Box 8.3* on p. 142.

3   Compare these résumés with your student's. Evaluate your student's résumé together, using the criteria developed in step 2.

4   Explain that you will divide the feedback into two stages: 1. general content, layout and organization; 2. grammar, vocabulary and style.

5   Ask your student to revise their résumé for homework and send it to you via email. They may want to use one of the templates available in Microsoft® Word or develop their own.

6   Provide feedback on the content, layout and organization in the next lesson (or provide written feedback via email). Identify positive features and suggest ways to improve it.

7   Ask your student to write a second draft for homework.

8   Provide detailed feedback on grammar, vocabulary and style. Identify positive points and suggestions for improvement.

9   When working on language, it may be helpful to discuss some positive action verbs to describe their work experience. For example: *made* ➔ *created, constructed, designed; helped* ➔ *facilitated, contributed, assisted; started* ➔ *established, implemented, initiated.*

10   Your student might want to try getting another opinion by showing the final version of their résumé to a friend or colleague and asking them to identify the most important points.

Technology option

Many job sites give the option of providing a link to an online résumé. This could be an interesting additional skill to work on together, or to ask your student to teach you using a program such as the Resume Builder (www.theresumebuilder.com/), My Resume Online (www.myresumeonline.org/) or VisualCV® (www.visualcv.com). Creating an online video résumé is another option (there are many examples on YouTube™). You may need to discuss with your student the possible risks of putting personal contact information on the Web.

Box 8.3: Improving your résumé

- What essential information will the employer or client look for first? Is it easy to find?
- Is the information ordered and presented logically?
- Does it look professional / serious / creative / friendly?
- What kind of headings / layout / fonts make it look interesting?
- Which words and expressions make it look interesting?
- What makes the résumé stand out from the crowd?

8.4 Conversation sampler

Outline	You and your student role play a conversation that they took part in recently. You record the role play and use the recording to give feedback on grammar, pronunciation and conversation strategies at different stages of the activity.
Focus	Social and interactional communicative skills
Level	Intermediate–Advanced
Time	30 minutes
Preparation	Bring in a portable recording device to your lesson.

Procedure

1   Discuss some of the situations when your student needs to use English in one-to-one interactions, perhaps with customers, clients or colleagues. You might choose to focus on short stereotypical situations such as greetings, arranging appointments or making requests.

2   Ask your student about a recent interaction and what happened.

3   Role play the conversation and record it.

4   Listen to the recording together. Ask your student to evaluate the interaction and say how they think it could be improved.

5   Then add your own feedback. You might give feedback first on grammar or pronunciation, then listen a second time and give feedback on conversation strategies.

6   Role play the interaction again, swapping roles and trying different options for responding.

Technology option

You might want to try recording a phone conversation between you and your student, or in a phone call via the internet by VoIP (e.g. Skype™), or via text messaging. Your student might also be able to record a real conversation they carried out with a customer on the phone or via text messaging online.

Variation

If your student does not currently use English in their job, use a conversation that they would normally carry out in their own language. This may yield insights into cultural differences. If you do not share your student's first language, this will also give them an opportunity to become your cultural informant, thereby incorporating real communicative purpose in the activity.

8.5 A job interview

Outline	You and your student work on developing a set of criteria for evaluating their job interview performance and use this to give feedback on their job interview skills.
Focus	Practising job interview skills
Level	Intermediate–Advanced
Time	40 minutes (but could be spread over several lessons)
Preparation	Assemble some links to websites that offer advice on job interviews on your desktop or smartboard, and send them to your student before the lesson. Make a copy of the job interview questionnaire in *Box 8.5a* (optional) and of the job interview evaluation checklist in *Box 8.5b* (optional). You can also find many webpages and videos relating to job interview tips online (search for 'job interview tips and mistakes').

Procedure

1 Start the lesson by asking your student about a job interview experience. You may want to use some of the questions used in the questionnaire (see *Box 8.5a*). Invite your student to ask you questions about your experiences, too.

2 Discuss what was common to your experiences and develop one or two tips for job interviewees. Or discuss the cultural differences between your experiences and those of your student and try to explain them.

3 Review the notes your student has taken for homework, or skim one or two sites together if you have internet access in your lesson.

4 Go back to the experiences you described in step 1. How could these tips have helped you?

5 Identify the type of job your student would be most likely to go to an interview for in the future. Work together on a set of questions that would be asked at such an interview. (This could also be set as homework.)

6 You could also sidetrack here into making a list of positive qualities that make your student ideally suited for such a job and that they would want to get across in an interview.

7 Use the questions you developed together in step 5 to interview your student. If possible, record the interview for later analysis.

8 Get some feedback from your student on how they felt about the interview. Help them to develop a set of criteria so that they can evaluate their own performance. This might include various categories such as Attitude, Knowledge, Experience (see *Box 8.5b* on p. 146 for examples).

9   Listen to the recording and ask your student to suggest ways to improve the overall tone and presentation of their interview. Then listen again and ask for any comments on grammar or vocabulary. Add your own feedback, remembering to include positive feedback as well as suggestions for improvement. (Your student could also transcribe part of it, as in *Activity 8.2: Transcribing a one-minute talk*.)

10 Repeat the interview, incorporating the improvements you have discussed.

11 For homework, ask your student to write a summary of the interviewing skills they need to improve, or to write a thank-you note to you (see the examples in *Boxes 8.5c* and *8.5d* on pp. 146–7).

Note
Encouraging your student to develop the interview questions and the evaluation criteria will make this activity especially relevant to them, as they promote and provide practice in skills that your student is likely to need to thrive in the real world.

Box 8.5a: A job interview

Job interview questionnaire

1 When was your last job interview?

   ....

2 What kind of job was the interview for?

   ....

3 What kinds of questions did they ask you?

   ....
   ....
   ....

4 What kinds of questions did you ask them?

   ....
   ....
   ....

5 Was it a successful interview? Why or why not?

   ....
   ....
   ....

From *Learning One-to-One* © Cambridge University Press 2010   PHOTOCOPIABLE

Box 8.5b: A job interview

Job interview evaluation criteria

Voice: loud? clear? ....

Attitude: enthusiastic? motivated? ....

Personality: confident? decisive? authoritative?..................................

Questions: clearly answered? appropriate knowledge demonstrated?
                        ....

Interpersonal skills: friendly? polite? cooperative? ....

From *Learning One-to-One* © Cambridge University Press 2010   PHOTOCOPIABLE

Box 8.5c: A job interview

Sample thank-you letter

21 Windsor Avenue
Winchester
Hampshire

Mr Arnold Wilson
Internet Investments Ltd
361 Pond Street
London

Dear Mr Wilson,

Thank you for taking the time to meet me and discuss the investment advisor position at your company. It was a pleasure to meet you and find out more about your company's operations.

After speaking with you, I am confident that my background and skills would enable me to make a significant contribution to your company.

I look forward to hearing from you very soon. Thank you again for your time and consideration.

Yours sincerely,

Anita Lewis

From *Learning One-to-One* © Cambridge University Press 2010   PHOTOCOPIABLE

Box 8.5d: A job interview

Sample thank-you email

To: A. Wilson
From: Anita Lewis
Subject: Thank You – Investment Advisor Interview

Dear Mr Wilson,

It was a pleasure to speak with you today about the investment advisor position at Internet Investments Inc.

I am confident that my background and skills would enable me to make a significant contribution to your company.

I look forward to hearing from you very soon.

Yours sincerely,

Anita Lewis
Email Address: alewis@internet.com
Phone Number: 4098-55889

From *Learning One-to-One* © Cambridge University Press 2010   PHOTOCOPIABLE

8.6 Leaving a phone message

Outline	You and your student work on developing a set of criteria for evaluating phone/voicemail messages and use this to give feedback on their phone message skills.
Focus	Practising the language of phone messages
Level	Intermediate–Advanced
Time	20–30 minutes
Preparation	Make some recordings of real phone or voicemail messages, or bring in examples from published materials (optional).

Procedure

1   Discuss with your student the kind of information that is required in a phone message. Make a list. It might be something like this:
   - who the message is for
   - the caller's name
   - the caller's number

- reason for calling
- action needed

2 Describe a situation where you need to leave a message for your student, such as when you want to cancel a lesson or have to change the date or time. For example:

> Your lesson is on Monday, and you want to change it to Tuesday.
> Your lesson is at 4 pm, and you want to change it to 4.30 pm.
> Your lesson is on Monday at 3 pm, but you will be ten minutes late.

3 Model a phone message that contains all the relevant points. Ask your student to check them off on the list. For example:

> Hi! This is Patricia. I'd like to leave a message for Elena. Our next lesson is on Monday, but I want to change it to Tuesday. Is that OK? Please call me back to confirm. My number is 650-456-1254. Thanks! Goodbye!

4 Now model a couple more messages, but leave something out. Your student will identify the missing information.

5 Try saying a message too fast, or mumbling a bit. Your student will say what is wrong. The idea is to encourage your student to give feedback to you so that they can better evaluate their own performance later.

6 Now work together to think of some more situations (your student can choose typical situations from their job or see *Variations* below) and ask your student to practise leaving a message.

7 If possible, record the messages and play them back. Is all the information included? Are they clear? Encourage your student to use the criteria they developed earlier, in step 1.

8 Listen to some recordings of phone messages (either authentic or from published materials), and ask your student to make notes of the relevant information using the checklist from step 1.

Variations

For business English, use situations from your student's workplace, e.g. requesting a meeting or an interview, cancelling a meeting, arranging a sales call.

8.7 Tricky situations

Outline	Your student describes a problem situation at work and you role play it with your student, giving you the opportunity to provide feedback on communication strategies, grammar and vocabulary.
Focus	Dealing with problem situations
Level	Intermediate–Advanced
Time	30 minutes
Preparation	None

Procedure

1 Brainstorm a list of difficult or tricky situations your student has encountered at work. For example, asking the manager to extend a deadline, apologizing to a customer for a delay in delivery, asking for a pay rise, asking for a vacation or a day off.

2 Ask your student to choose one of these situations to role play.

3 Discuss what happened in this situation. Decide on your role and discuss any extra background information that you need to play your role.

4 Role play the situation, imitating what happened as best you can. Then switch roles and replay.

5 Discuss positive aspects of the interaction. Then discuss what aspects of the interaction could be improved in order to get a better result. You may divide the feedback into two stages: in the first stage focus on pragmatic strategies and, if appropriate, cultural differences; in the second stage, focus on grammatical accuracy and vocabulary.

6 Role play the situation again.

Variations

1 Use 'emotion/personality' cards (see *Box 6.7a* on p. 111) to vary the interaction some more. For example, the manager could be 'angry' and the employee could be 'confident' or 'assertive'.

2 Record the 'before' and 'after' conversations to see how different they were.

8.8 Listen to the gaps

Outline	You read aloud a text with some missing words. Your student tries to guess the missing words, enabling you to provide instant feedback on their guesses.
Focus	Developing listening skills
Level	Low intermediate–Advanced
Time	20 minutes
Preparation	Find a short text suitable for dictation.

Procedure

1   After reading a text together, ask your student to choose one part of the text for a type of dictation. (Or choose a short text relevant to your student's needs such as the one in *Box 8.8a* and read it aloud once.)

2   Read the text aloud again, but this time 'gap' some easily guessed words by saying 'beep' or using some other signal (see *Boxes 8.8b* and *8.8c*). These will usually be grammar words, such as prepositions or auxiliary verbs, or articles (but this may be very difficult). The idea is to choose words that students could guess from the surrounding sentence.

3   Pause at the end of the group of words to let your student say the missing word. You can give feedback immediately by smiling or frowning and allow your student several guesses, giving hints such as 'It's a preposition' if needed. If they cannot work it out, you can 'mouth' or whisper the word to help them.

4   Read the text again, but gap some different words.

5   At the end, your student may be ready to reconstruct the entire text from memory.

Box 8.8a: Listen to the gaps

Dear Sir,

Due to reasons beyond our control, we regret to inform you that there will be a two-week delay in the shipment of the above order. Thank you for your understanding.

Sincerely,
Andrew Johnson

Box 8.8b: Listen to the gaps

Dear Sir,

Due (beep) reasons beyond our control, we regret (beep) inform you that there will be a two-week delay in the shipment (beep) the above order. Thank you (beep) your understanding.

Sincerely,
Andrew Johnson

Box 8.8c: Listen to the gaps

Dear (beep),

Due to (beep) beyond our control, we (beep) to inform you that there will be a two-week (beep) in the shipment of the above order. Thank you for (beep) understanding.

(beep),
Andrew Johnson

This idea is adapted from *Teaching Listening Comprehension* by Penny Ur, Cambridge University Press 1984.

8.9 Writing a business letter

Outline	You and your student analyse some examples of business letters and compare them with one they have written.
Focus	Developing business letter-writing skills
Level	Intermediate–Advanced
Time	30 minutes
Preparation	Ask your student for a copy of a business letter they have written. Prepare a model business letter cut up into strips (see *Box 8.9a*). Prepare a blank diagram outline of a business letter (see *Box 8.9b* on p. 154).

Procedure

1   Give your student the strips of the business letter to sequence in the correct order.

2   Read the letter together and describe the various sections of the letter. Discuss the differences between an informal letter and a business letter.

3   Read your student's letter and try to match the parts of the letter and other stylistic features. Say what is the same and what is different.

4   Give feedback on the letter (overall content and organization first, then grammar and vocabulary) and discuss how it could be improved.

5   Elicit some other situations when your student has to write business letters. Make a list.

6   Choose one of them to work on in your lesson. Use a template such as the one in *Box 8.9b*, or one from Microsoft® Word.

7   Choose another situation from the list for homework.

Technology option

For homework, or before the lesson, ask your student to look at online resources for writing business letters (see, e.g., www.esl.about.com/library/howto/htbusiness.htm or owl.english.purdue.edu/owl/resource/653/01/).

Box 8.9a: Writing a business letter

Solar Energy Panels Co.
45 Pound Lane
Wakefield, Yorkshire
WF5 671

Tel: 566-9055
Fax: 567-908862
Email: dan@sunnyenergy.com

3 September

Mr Alan Robinson
Manager, Windy Hill Hotel
65 Windy Hill Road
Wakefield, Yorkshire
WF2 676

Dear Mr Robinson,

With reference to our telephone conversation today, I am writing to confirm your order for ten solar energy panels.

The order will be shipped within three days and should arrive within two weeks.

Please do not hesitate to contact us again if we can provide any further assistance.

Yours sincerely,

Alex Minton

Alex Minton
Director of Solar Energy Panels Co.

Box 8.9b: Writing a business letter

Your name and address

Addressee's name and address

Date

Salutation

Subject of letter

Main message

Closing remarks

Signature

Printed name and job title

From *Learning One-to-One* © Cambridge University Press 2010   PHOTOCOPIABLE

8.10 Communication style

Outline	You and your student analyse some examples of emails they have written and discuss stylistic features of emails compared with formal letters or phone calls. This gives you the opportunity to provide feedback on the style, content and format of their emails.
Focus	Developing email writing skills
Level	Low intermediate–Advanced
Time	20–30 minutes
Preparation	Ask your student for some examples of emails they have sent and some replies they have received recently.

Procedure

1 Read the emails that you or your student has brought to the lesson. If you have a few examples, ask your student to choose the pair of emails they are most interested in.

2 Ask your student to explain who the emails are from, who they are to, what the main topic is and what the tone of the correspondence is.

3 Identify any features of the message that are specific to emails, e.g. the salutation, the closing, the use of short, direct sentences. See the example in *Box 8.10* on p. 156.

4 Give feedback on the style of the emails your student has brought in. Do they seem formal or informal and why? What kind of response would they tend to elicit?

5 Discuss ways of making the emails more or less formal.

6 Now use the information from steps 4 and 5 to turn the emails into a phone conversation. Discuss some of the aspects that are different from an email. Then switch roles and role play again.

7 Finally, discuss how to turn the phone call into a formal letter, again noting the stylistic differences needed for formal letter writing in contrast to informal emails. This can be set for homework.

Variations

1 This activity can be adapted for non-business contexts, e.g. complaining about a product, or about a delivery delay, or about an excessive gas bill.

2 You could also try having a conversation with your student via short messages (using Twitter, for example, or using abbreviations common in text messaging) and turn them into a spoken conversation or summarize them into a longer email.

Technology option

Look up websites that give advice on email etiquette (search for 'email etiquette rules and tips') and compile a list of the top ten tips.

Box 8.10: Communication style

To: Scott
From: Jim
Subject: New QA software system

Hi Scott:

Any updates on the new QA software system?
Please advise asap.

Thanks
Jim

8.11 Email follow-up

Outline	Use some personal information that your student has shared with you to send an email following up on the grammar point you studied in your lesson. Their reply will allow you to give feedback on how well they have used the target grammar.
Focus	Consolidating target language studied in your last lesson
Level	Elementary–Advanced
Time	20 minutes

Procedure

1 During the lesson, make a note of some information about the student that you would like to hear more about and which could encourage the student to use the target language. For example, you may notice that they have mentioned starting a new sport or evening class.

2 After the lesson, send an email reminding them about this topic, asking for their opinion and linking it to the previously studied area of grammar or vocabulary (see the example on the topic of comparisons in *Box 8.11*). The email serves a dual function: it is communicative and it practises the target language of your lesson.

3   Use the information in the email to start off your next lesson and review language from the previous lesson.

Note

This is a simple strategy for reminding students of the language areas they studied with you in the previous lesson, guiding them to establish good study habits. Their reply to your email provides some material for use in your next lesson or to keep as a record of your student's learning progress.

Box 8.11: Email follow-up

To: Andrea
From: Sarah
Subject: Your new yoga class

Hi Andrea,

Last time you mentioned you were going to try out a new yoga class. What is it like? Is it better than your other class, or not as good?
Talk to you soon,

Sarah

8.12 Learning from mistakes

Outline	Discuss with your student the best way for you to give them feedback. This will help to improve mutual understanding of teacher/student expectations and encourage learner reflection on how feedback helps them to learn.
Focus	Any
Level	Intermediate–Advanced
Time	20 minutes
Preparation	Make a copy of the questionnaire in *Box 8.12*.

Procedure

1 Explain that you are going to discuss the best way to approach mistakes so that it will help your student learn.

2 Use the questionnaire in *Box 8.12* (adapted for your own context as needed) to start off a discussion about how to handle corrections in your lessons.

3 The aim of the activity is to come up with a few general rules (that can be changed later) and see how they work in practice.

Note

As there is a greater need for accuracy in writing than in speaking, it is worth making two separate 'rules' for written and spoken language, but you may also want to differentiate free from formal speaking and writing.

Box 8.12: Learning from mistakes

1 Writing
In my written homework, I would like the teacher to . . .
- ❏ correct all my mistakes
- ❏ only correct the most serious mistakes
- ❏ underline the mistakes and I'll try to correct them
- ❏ underline the mistakes and tell me what kind of mistake it is (grammar, spelling, etc.)
- ❏ (other) ....

In my written homework, I would like to . . .
- ❏ discuss all the corrections with my teacher
- ❏ try to work out the mistakes and ask questions if I have problems
- ❏ rewrite the homework, correcting all the mistakes
- ❏ rewrite only the sentences with mistakes
- ❏ (other) ....

2 Speaking
When I am speaking, I would like the teacher to . . .
- ❏ correct all my mistakes
- ❏ only correct mistakes when he/she cannot understand something
- ❏ write down the mistakes and I'll try to correct them
- ❏ point out the mistakes and tell me what kind of mistake it is (grammar, pronunciation, etc.)
- ❏ (other) ....

When I am speaking, I would like to . . .
- ❏ focus on making every sentence correct (accuracy)
- ❏ focus on sounding natural and fluent (fluency)
- ❏ focus on communicating well (communication)
- ❏ focus sometimes on accuracy, and sometimes on fluency
- ❏ (other) ....

From *Learning One-to-One* © Cambridge University Press 2010   PHOTOCOPIABLE

This idea is adapted from *Treatment of Error in Second Language Student Writing* by Dana R. Ferris, The University of Michigan Press 2002.

Mentor and guide

The activities in this chapter focus on the role of the teacher as mentor and guide (see *Chapter 2*, pp. 32–4). An awareness of this role directs attention away from language per se to language learning strategies. The following activities provide opportunities to advise and support the learner and help them develop independent learning skills. They can be used to encourage your student to try out new study strategies and tools for learning, as well as to reflect on existing strategies.

9.1 Independent learning checklist

Outline	Your student reflects on how they learn out of class and develops their range of out-of-class learning strategies.
Focus	Talking about routines (*where do you usually . . .?*) and making suggestions (*you could . . . you should . . . how about . . .?*)
Level	Intermediate–Advanced
Time	20–30 minutes
Preparation	None

Procedure

1 Ask your student to tell you about ways that they learn English out of class.

2 Make a list of these or write them in a brainstorm pattern scattered around the board or paper.

3 Work together on ways to organize the ideas. They might be best organized according to skill (speaking, listening, reading, writing) or according to whether they are usually done at home, at work, online or at school.

4 Create a chart to show these different categories. (See *Box 9.1* for an example.)

5 Think of additional ideas and add them to each section (as shown in italics in *Box 9.1*).

6 You may find it helpful to ask some of the following questions:

- What kinds of websites are good for learning English?
- What grammar reference book (or website) do you recommend?

- What kind of dictionary (print or online) do you use? Why do you like it?
- Where can you meet English-speaking people (face-to-face or online)?
- What are some good ways of recording and reviewing vocabulary?
- What are some good ways of increasing vocabulary?

7   Finally, work together to start compiling a list of useful websites for learning English. Your student may already know some, and you can ask why they like these websites and what they use them for. You can use this information to set homework tasks. (A list of useful websites is given in the *Websites* section on pp. 202–3.)

8   The chart and the list of websites can be added to your student's portfolio.

Note

This is a useful way of building up a list of strategies for learning out of class employing a combination of different skills that expand on the strategies they already use and that work well for them.

Box 9.1: Independent learning checklist

Speaking	Listening
Speak with customers from other countries Speak with my American friends *Phone my teacher* *Join an online learning community*	Listen to the BBC news on the radio Listen to English songs Watch English films *Listen to podcasts online (newspaper or BBC)* *Go to lectures at the British Council*

Reading	Writing
Read the newspaper Read short stories or novels Use my *English–English* dictionary	Write emails to my teacher Do my homework *Write in my language learning blog or diary* *Write new words in my vocabulary notebook*

9.2 Vocabulary ping-pong

Outline	Your student tries out a strategy for remembering vocabulary.
Focus	Practising recall of synonyms and antonyms
Level	Beginner–Elementary
Time	5–10 minutes
Preparation	Bring a ball or beanbag for throwing.

Procedure

1 Identify a set of adjectives and their opposites that you have already studied quite thoroughly, e.g. *strong/weak*, *rich/poor*, *tall/short*, etc. Review them if necessary. Add a few more that are less familiar.
2 You will say an adjective and throw the ball (or beanbag).
3 Your student will catch the ball and say the opposite, and then throw the ball back to you.
4 Keep playing until you run out of adjectives.

Note

The activity focuses on the strategy of improving vocabulary by connecting words with their synonyms and antonyms. You may suggest that your student looks up synonyms and antonyms when recording new words in their vocabulary notebook, or when making sets of vocabulary cards for review.

Variations

Instead of using adjectives and their antonyms, try synonyms, phrasal verbs and their synonyms, verbs in past and present tense, or verbs and past participles.

9.3 Phrasal verbs

Outline	Your student tries out a strategy for remembering phrasal verbs.
Focus	Using phrasal verbs with and without pronouns in short dialogues
Level	Intermediate and above
Time	15–20 minutes
Preparation	Prepare a set of cards with phrasal verbs and their one-word synonyms that you have studied (or see *Box 9.3* on p. 164).

Procedure

1 Review the meanings of the phrasal verbs by matching them with their synonyms.

2 Go over the rules of phrasal verbs (separable v. inseparable, and rules with object pronouns).

3 Spread the cards out on the table. Explain that you are going to ask a question using the synonym and your student will reply using the phrasal verb and the appropriate pronoun. For example:

Teacher: Have they postponed the meeting?
Student: Yes, they have put it off until next week.

4 Each time your student successfully completes the dialogue, they can take the pair of cards.

5 Spread the cards out on the table again. This time your student will ask the questions using the phrasal verbs, and you will answer using the one-word synonym. For example

Student: Have they put off the meeting?
Teacher: Yes, they have postponed it until next week.

6 Order the phrasal verbs according to how frequently your student thinks they would use them in their workplace conversations or communications.

7 Write workplace examples of similar dialogues for the top five phrasal verbs.

8 Use these dialogues for review in your next lesson.

Note

This activity could be used to encourage your student to use vocabulary cards to review vocabulary out of class. You might suggest that they make their own set of cards based on this activity, with phrasal verbs on one side and one-word synonyms on the other. Another idea is to write sentences with gaps for the phrasal verb and write the missing verb on the back.

Box 9.3: Phrasal verbs

postpone	put off	visit	call on	investigate	look into
cancel	call off	resemble	take after	invent	make up
donate	give away	prepare	get ready	remove	take away
distribute	give out	review	go over	discover	come across
fail	break down	suggest	put forward	start	set up
return	get back	leave	set off	escape	get away

✂

From *Learning One-to-One* © Cambridge University Press 2010   PHOTOCOPIABLE

9.4 True friends and false friends

Outline	Your student develops strategies for avoiding vocabulary errors with false friends.
Focus	Identifying cognates and false friends
Level	Intermediate–Advanced
Time	20–30 minutes
Preparation	Prepare a list of words that are similar in English and in your student's first language, if possible recycling words that have come up in your recent lessons. Some of them should be real cognates and some false friends (i.e. they look similar but are different in meaning). Write each one on a small card.

Procedure

1 Explain the difference between a cognate and a false friend.
2 Mix up the cards and put them on the table.
3 Ask your student to sort them into two piles.

4   For the cognates, mention any differences in pronunciation or spelling.

5   For the false friends, give examples of sentences where they are used differently. Use a dictionary to help you.

6   Now sort the false friends into two piles – ones that are difficult to remember and ones that are easy.

7   For the words in the difficult pile, work on preparing sentences with gaps that will illustrate the meaning of the word. If possible, create example sentences related to true information about your student.

8   Use the sentences to create a set of vocabulary cards for your student to review out of class. Write the sentences with gaps on one side and the missing words on the other.

9   Brainstorm other strategies for remembering the differences in meaning.

Notes

1   Some useful lists of false friends can be found in *Learner English: A Teacher's Guide to Interference and Other Problems* (Second edition), edited by Michael Swan and Bernard Smith, Cambridge University Press 2001.

2   If you do not share your student's first language, this activity gives them an opportunity to teach you about the meanings of these words in their own language.

9.5 Test-taking tips and strategies

Outline	Your student reflects on test-taking strategies and expands their range of test-taking skills.
Focus	Test-taking
Level	Intermediate–Advanced
Time	20 minutes
Preparation	Make a copy of a test that has one example of each question type, e.g. multiple-choice, true/false, fill the gaps, etc.

Procedure

1   Choose an example (or create a shortened version) of a test that has several different question types.

2   Explain that you are going to have a lesson about test-taking strategies, but first you are going to try out a test.

3   Allow five minutes for your student to complete the test.

4   Now go back to the first question and ask your student to tell you how they approached the question. Did they read the question first and then all the answers? Did they read the question and then try to predict the answer before reading the answers? Did they read all the answers and eliminate all the wrong ones?

5   You may find it helpful to ask your student to complete a chart for each question type as you go along, first filling out your student's preferred method, then adding others, as in *Box 9.5*.

6   For homework, ask your student to look at some websites for test-taking tips on the internet and collect ten more useful tips for the next lesson.

Note

Most students use some kind of test-taking strategies, even though they may not realize what they are. This activity encourages your student to verbalize the strategies they use and to consider some possible alternatives. As tests are generally seen as result-oriented rather than process-oriented, some students may be reluctant to explore this topic, and their perception of its value could influence whether you decide to continue with the activity.

Variation

An alternative way to approach this is to model a short demonstration of how to verbalize your strategies. For example, you can look at the first question and say, 'I'm reading the directions carefully first. It says that one answer is wrong. Now I'm reading the question and I'm trying to think of the correct answer. Now I'm reading the answer choices. I'm reading all of them carefully before I decide', and so on. Once your student has understood what you want, they can take over the verbalization process.

Technology option

Many sample tests can be found online, including sample tests and test-taking tips for the Cambridge ESOL examinations, IELTS and TOEFL. It might be helpful to discuss some differences between taking tests on paper and on computer. Some web resources for test-taking tips can be found in the *Websites* section on pp. 202–3.

Box 9.5: Test-taking tips and strategies

Type of test question	My strategies	Additional strategies
Multiple-choice	Read directions and questions carefully. Read all the choices before choosing the answer. Eliminate answers I am sure are wrong.	Try to think of the answer first before looking at the possible answers. Answer easy questions first.
True/false		
Correct the mistakes		
Fill the gaps		

9.6 Pronunciation ranking

Outline	Your student develops systematic strategies for tackling pronunciation problems.
Focus	Any
Level	Beginner–Advanced
Time	10–15 minutes
Preparation	None

Procedure

1 Based on your analysis of your student's pronunciation needs, identify an area of pronunciation work (specific phonemes) that needs more intensive practice.

2 Start with a dictation of words that contain two easily confused sounds (e.g. words with voiced and unvoiced *th*). Ask your student to write them under the correct heading (see *Box 9.6* on p. 168 for an example).

3 Identify the easiest and the most difficult words in the group and rank them in order of difficulty.

4 Focus on the mechanics of producing the target sound if needed. (See the *References and further reading* section, pp. 200–1, for books on pronunciation. There are also demonstration videos on YouTube™.)

5 Work with your student to create example sentences containing the target words that have personal meaning. For example:

> I have *three* sisters. My birthday is on the *thirteenth* of August.

6   If you have a recording device, take turns recording these sentences on audio, you first, and your student afterwards.

7   For homework, record the words and the sentences with gaps so that your student can listen again at home and record their voice after yours (this gives them the opportunity to practise multiple times at home and choose the best examples to bring to the next lesson).

Variations
You can also use this activity to practise recognizing the number of syllables in a word or different syllable stress patterns.

Note
Many online dictionaries have an audio recording for each word entry. There are many pronunciation practice programs you can buy online or on CD where you can practise listening to individual words and record your own voice for comparison, including the *Cambridge Pronouncing Dictionary CD-ROM*.

Box 9.6: Pronunciation ranking

Words containing 'th'	Words not containing 'th'
2 three	1 tree
3 mouth	4 mouse
6 think	5 sink

9.7 Using your skills

Outline	Your student reflects on skills they already have that can help them in language learning.
Focus	Describing skills, e.g. *be good at/with ...*, *be able to ...*, *know how to ...*
Level	Intermediate–Advanced
Time	20–30 minutes
Preparation	None

Procedure

1   Ask your student to make a list of all the skills they use in their job, and the personal characteristics and past experiences that help them to do it. See *Box 9.7* for some examples.

2   Discuss which of these skills are useful for learning English. For example, being able to use the internet means you can use English learning websites, online dictionaries, etc.

3   Ask your student to write a paragraph or two for homework about how they apply their skills to learning English. You could also choose one aspect of their experience, e.g. playing volleyball, and say how learning to play volleyball is like or unlike learning English.

Note

This activity could be used as a confidence booster if your student starts to feel discouraged about lack of progress.

Box 9.7: Using your skills

Skills I use in my job	Personal characteristics that are useful for my job	Past experience that helps me in my job
How to use the internet	determined, persistent	Lived abroad when I was young
How to communicate with customers	patient, optimistic	Member of volleyball team when I was at school

From *Learning One-to-One* © Cambridge University Press 2010   PHOTOCOPIABLE

9.8 Visiting Second Life®

Outline	Your student learns about how to use a virtual world such as Second Life for independent language learning.
Focus	Any
Level	Any
Time	Flexible
Preparation	It is advisable to familiarize yourself with how to download the program and how to use the tools available in Second Life before trying them in your lesson.

Procedure

1   If your student has not come across Second Life (www.secondlife.com), explain that it is a virtual world which is accessible via the internet. Visitors can select an avatar (a character) which can move around the Second Life world and interact with other avatars. They can communicate with each other

via text chat or voice. They can explore, meet other residents, participate in individual and group activities, and travel throughout the world.

2 Make sure both your and your student's computers have the necessary system requirements for downloading the program.

3 Download the Second Life program and set up an avatar. Practise moving around with your avatar. If you and your student plan to do this from the same physical location (i.e. not as a distance learning tool), this may be a good thing for your student to teach you, or for you to teach your student, as it would generate a lot of instructional language.

4 Here are a few ideas for activities that will help your student use Second Life for their independent learning:

- **Go on a field trip.** Visit a museum or an art exhibit. Visit famous cities such as Berlin or Paris. Go to the supermarket or the zoo. Go to a café or a restaurant. While you walk around, name the things you see, or exchange opinions about them. When your student goes there on their own, they can give you their evaluation or recommend places for you to visit and say why.

- **Visit language learning communities.** Such locations include the English Village (slurl.com/secondlife/English Village) and the British Council Island (http://slurl.com/secondlife/British Council Isle). Second Life English (www.slenglish.ning.com) has a mix of teachers and students. Another interesting community for those who want to practise a language and are willing to teach one in exchange is Teach You Teach Me (www.teachyouteachme.ning.com). Your first trip to these places may be to research and evaluate the opportunities being offered there for English language learning. Your student can then decide if they want to return and what they want to do there.

- **Go on a webquest.** After visiting Second Life together, your student may come up with some ideas of places they want to explore on their own. You could prepare a webquest based on their choices. A first task might be to find out about language learning opportunities in the English Village, for example. Another might be to find out what kinds of exhibits are on display in a museum. Your student can write a report or tell you what they have found out in your next lesson.

- **Explore sites for experts.** Find communities that have sites related to your student's field of specialization, e.g. business, medicine or law. They can search for other communities (or groups) in Second Life which have nothing to do with language learning directly, but with their interests. They can then attend group meetings or get alerts about interesting events, which are mostly free to participate in.
- **Carry out a survey.** Help your student develop an idea for a survey they can carry out in Second Life. Your student can ask as many people as possible and compile a report about their views. Be aware, though, that not everybody will be willing to participate in a survey and questions should be chosen carefully. Questions about real-life identity, for example, should not be asked.
- **Make a copy of a text-chat conversation.** Students can copy the text-chat conversation or have it automatically logged and stored on their computer. This can be used later as a basis for work on grammar, vocabulary, formality or appropriateness. Audio recordings are also possible (with additional software). Text and audio recordings should not be made without the permission of all participants. In all cases, be careful to protect the privacy of recorded conversations (i.e. they should not be made public).

Notes

1   Joining Second Life is free and there are a lot of free resources for educators. (You have to pay if you want some of the additional functionalities, but they are not essential.)
2   Second Life is for adults only and for teenagers there is Teen Second Life (www.teen.secondlife.com).
3   The Second Life website offers a PDF guide on getting started (see www.secondlife.com/support/). Other step-by-step guides for getting started can be found online. See, for example, http://wiki.sla.org/display/ SLASECONDLIFE/Getting+started+in+Second+Life.
4   There are also other virtual worlds that you might want to investigate for their possible potential for language learning, e.g. Twinity (www.twinity.com).

Many thanks to Nergiz Kern for contributing her ideas and insights on teaching English in Second Life to this activity.

9.9 Designing listening comprehension questions

Outline	Your student creates questions for an audio or video segment in order to develop strategies for active listening, as well as improving their listening skills.
Focus	Asking questions, listening skills
Level	Beginner and above
Time	30 minutes
Preparation	Select an audio or video segment on a topic related to your student's interests at the same or lower language level than your learner's level.

Procedure

1 Introduce the topic of the audio. Try to predict some of the vocabulary from the title or the topic.

2 Explain that in today's lesson you are going to switch roles, and that your student is going to ask the questions.

3 Listen to the audio and ask your student to prepare and write down three or four questions about the content.

4 Correct or clarify the questions if necessary. Answer them. If necessary, listen again to check the answers. (How did you do? Let your student evaluate you.)

5 Notice the types of questions your learner created. Were they mostly fact-based, opinion-based, grammar- or vocabulary-based? Listen again and ask your student to develop further questions in the missing categories.

6 Finally, you may want to work together to develop questions about things that were implied in or omitted from the audio. These questions can be set for homework.

Note

This activity may require some patience. Even though it may not work well at first, it is worth making the effort to centre this activity completely on the learner's questions so that the next time you use a listening text, your student will feel more able to collaborate in the questioning/learning process.

9.10 Listen and summarize

Outline	Your student listens to you reading an article aloud in order develop note-taking and summarizing skills.
Focus	Practising note-taking and summarizing skills
Level	Intermediate–Advanced
Time	30 minutes
Preparation	Bring in a short text (from a newspaper, magazine, the internet or a coursebook) related to your student's professional/academic field. The text should contain some new information, but most of the vocabulary should be very familiar.

Procedure

1 Explain that you are going to use this lesson to practise note-taking and summarizing skills.

2 Read the text aloud. Your student takes notes in English or in their own language.

3 Go over your student's notes and highlight some good points about their note-taking skills. Suggest one or two improvements, e.g. using symbols or abbreviations, or using a different layout.

4 Record your student as they give an oral summary of the text.

5 Your student can use the recording to write a summary for homework.

6 You and your student compare the written summary and the text in the next lesson.

Variation

While your student is talking, you can highlight the facts that were mentioned in the oral summary (this can be done with coloured markers on an interactive whiteboard or using an editing tool). Afterwards, decide if any important facts were left out.

9.11 Choosing a story

Outline	Your student creates questions based on a text in order to develop strategies for active reading, as well as improving their reading skills.
Focus	Asking questions
Level	Beginner and above
Time	20–40 minutes
Preparation	Bring in a selection of short articles from magazines or newspapers.

Procedure

1 Choose a selection of articles that you think will interest your student, perhaps current affairs or something related to their job or country, or ask your student to bring some in.
2 Each of you will choose a different article, the one that you find most interesting.
3 Allow three or four minutes for silent reading.
4 You and your student will write three or four questions about the article.
5 Exchange articles and questions. Allow time for silent reading.
6 Answer the questions (either verbally or in writing).
7 Evaluate each other's answers to the questions.
8 Discuss any points of interest that came up during the activity.
9 You might ask your student to read the article again at home and talk about it in the next class, write a summary, or send a response by email.

Notes

1 Giving your student the opportunity to select material for study increases their participation in the learning process and can help motivation.
2 Writing questions about a text is often a good way of evaluating comprehension, but it also helps to reveal what your student would like to talk about in the article. The questions might be quite different from those you would have prepared yourself.

9.12 Guessing words from context

Outline	Your student reads an article and identifies key words in order to develop strategies for guessing words from context.
Focus	Identifying key words and guessing their meaning
Level	Intermediate–Advanced
Time	20–40 minutes
Preparation	Bring in a short article from a magazine, newspaper or from the internet.

Procedure

1 Choose an article that has a fairly low number of new vocabulary items.

2 Ask your student to read the article and circle five words that are unfamiliar to them. If possible, they should be words that they feel are key to understanding the article.

3 When your student is ready, go over the words they have chosen, trying to use the context to work out the meaning, and perhaps using a dictionary to support or disprove their conclusions. (Consulting a dictionary will bring in other skills, e.g. judging which definitions fit the context.)

4 As you are doing this, help your student to verbalize the strategies they are using.

5 Ask your student to arrange the five words in order of difficulty and speculate on why they were difficult (e.g. because there weren't enough context clues, or perhaps the word was colloquial or being used figuratively).

6 Encourage your student to reflect on the strategies they used successfully to work out the meaning. Your student can start making a list of these strategies in their notebook. Some examples of strategies might be: noticing if the word is defined in context, if any synonyms or antonyms are used in the surrounding text, or if any examples are given that could help define the meaning.

7 Next time you may ask your student to do this activity for homework (using an article of their choice) and discuss the key words in your lesson.

Technology option

If you are teaching online, ask your student to highlight the words in the text in colour. They can write definitions of the words in this context. They can highlight the context clues in a different colour to show how they worked out the meaning.

9.13 Timed skim-reading

Outline	Your student chooses a text to read quickly in order to reflect on their strategies for skim-reading.
Focus	Skim-reading
Level	Intermediate–Advanced
Time	20–40 minutes
Preparation	Bring in a selection of readers or a magazine.

Procedure

1 Ask your student to choose a reader or an article from a magazine. You choose one too.

2 Set a time limit of three minutes to find out as much about the article or book as you can.

3 After three minutes, write as much as you can about the book or article. For example, here is the result of reading the first few pages of a reader *The Secret Agent* by Joseph Conrad (Penguin Readers, Level 3):

> The setting is Victorian London. The characters seem mysterious. The owner Mr Verloc has mysterious visitors. And a strange son. How are these connected? What are the meetings about? What is his wife's role?

4 Read your written work aloud to each other and ask each other further questions.

5 Decide if you would like to continue reading this book or article in more detail.

6 Reflect on and compare the strategies you used for skimming information in the reading material. Did you look at headings and captions? First line and last line? A few words in each line?

7 Lead into a discussion of different strategies for skim-reading and how they can be used for selecting reading material.

This idea is adapted from 'Two Writing Activities for Extensive Reading' by Richard R. Day, *English Teaching Forum* 42(3) 2004.

9.14 Going on a webquest

Outline	Your student uses a variety of research skills to find information from the internet and compiles the information to complete a task and present a report.
Focus	Developing internet research skills, exploring the internet as a resource for language learning
Level	Low intermediate and above
Time	15–30 minutes, plus independent study time
Preparation	Prepare a webquest or choose one from the examples below.

Procedure

1   Explain that your student is going to complete a task by doing some research on the internet. They have to look at a variety of websites to find the information. The answers are not fixed but must all be based on real information available on the Web.

2   You may want to discuss with your student the different types of webquests they could do (see examples in *Boxes 9.14a* and *9.14b* on p. 178) and ask them to choose one they are interested in. Or you might want to start off with just one question, or a set of questions, and gradually build up to more complex tasks. Webquests can also be used to simulate real-life research tasks that the student may have to do for work or study.

3   Having chosen the webquest you are interested in, discuss some strategies for finding the information, e.g. what types of sites would be helpful, what keywords you could use. If you have access to the internet, start off by looking up a couple of sites together.

4   In the next lesson, go over the information they have compiled. If appropriate, ask your student to do a short presentation. A written report can be added to their portfolio.

5   You may choose to extend the activity into a role play or a letter-writing activity.

6   An important part of the rationale for doing webquests is that they enable students to develop skills of evaluating information they find on the Web. You can help them to do this by asking their opinion of the reliability of the sites they visited. Who produced them? Are they trustworthy sources? Did the student find conflicting information? Why does this happen? How can this issue be resolved?

7   Finally, help your student to reflect on the skills they developed by doing this activity and ask them to write a summary of these skills in their journal or portfolio.

Note

Some resources for webquests can be found in the *Websites* section on pp. 202–3.

Box 9.14a: Going on a webquest

Example tasks

1 Choose two musicals (exhibitions, concerts, movies, plays) showing in London right now. Write down the names, the theatre addresses, the cost of the tickets. What is the show about? Which one do you want to go to and why?

2 Plan a three-day trip for yourself to New York City. Find the flight, hotel, restaurant for dinner, an art exhibition and a concert or play. Create the itinerary and calculate the total cost for one person.

3 You want to visit Sydney for three days to see all the famous sights. Plan a three-day trip and decide what to visit on each day.

Box 9.14b: Going on a webquest

Example projects

1 Find out about a traditional festival (Halloween, Thanksgiving or Guy Fawkes). What does it celebrate? Where is it celebrated? What are the origins of the festival? What kind of food is eaten? What kinds of activities take place?

2 Find out about three companies (car, computer, electronics, supermarket) in the UK. How big are they? How many stores or factories do they have? How are they different and similar to each other and to similar companies in your country?

3 Research competitors' products in the UK or the USA. Do they have an identical product? How is it similar or different? What is the pricing plan?

9.15 Problem-solving

Outline	You and your student brainstorm solutions to problems in order to reflect on strategies and develop creative approaches to problem-solving.
Focus	Practising modals: *should, could, might, ought to, had better. You should do x, otherwise y might happen* and conditionals: *If you do x, y will happen*
Level	Intermediate–Advanced
Time	20–30 minutes
Preparation	None

Procedure

1 Ask your student to describe a typical problem that they have to face at work. It might be a problem with a supplier, a contractor, an employee or a co-worker, for example. Take notes and ask questions as you listen.

2 You in turn will also describe a typical problem that you face in your work (or in a previous job if more appropriate). Make sure your student gets plenty of opportunity to ask questions about the background and details of the problem.

3 Allow a few minutes of quiet thinking time for each of you to note down as many different solutions to the problem as you can think of. If you have time, number them in order of preference.

4 Exchange papers and read the suggested solutions carefully. Allow time to read them all and think about them before discussing.

5 Encourage your student to take a creative approach, looking for the positive aspect of any suggestion and considering how it might be incorporated into an alternative solution. For example:

> Problem: Employee does not finish work on time.
> Solution: Send employee to time-management classes.
> Negative response: We don't have time or money for that.
> Positive response: I could give her some tips on how to manage her time.

6 Incorporate the positive elements of these suggestions and try to combine them into one solution. You may focus on grammar here, e.g. *you should/could . . .; You'd better; If you do x, y will happen.*

7 Try to identify how your approaches to problems were similar or different. Use your discussion to come up with ways of evaluating problem-solving. For example, were they empathy-oriented, logical, creative, cooperative, collaborative, decisive, authoritarian? This may lead into a discussion of cultural or company values and how this affects the ways in which problems are solved.

10 Learner

The activities in this chapter focus on the role of the teacher as learner (see *Chapter 2*, pp. 34–5). Awareness of this role allows your student to take over some of the responsibility for the lesson and facilitates a more collaborative approach to your lessons; this, in turn, will generate a natural exchange of language as you make decisions together about your lessons. The following activities give the learner an opportunity to tell or teach you something. They exploit the natural information gap that exists between an expert and a non-expert in a particular field, and they give the learner the opportunity to take on some degree of authority which may boost their confidence and help to equalize the power relationship between teacher and student.

10.1 Your education

Outline	Your student describes the education system in their country to you and their experience and opinion of it.
Focus	Vocabulary for describing education
Level	Low intermediate–Advanced
Time	20–30 minutes
Preparation	Make a copy of a diagram of the educational system in England (see *Box 10.1a*) or the USA (see *Box 10.1b* on p. 182).

Procedure

1 Use the diagram in *Box 10.1a* or *Box 10.1b* to introduce vocabulary related to different types of schools and school systems. You may want to print out the diagram with some blanks so that students can ask you questions to fill it in.

2 Ask your student to ask you questions about the system, e.g. *At what age do children start primary school in England?* Encourage additional questions such as *Which years are compulsory? What subjects do you study?* etc. Make a list of useful vocabulary as you go along.

3 Ask your student to describe the education system in their country so that you can draw a similar diagram. (If you share your student's culture, skip steps 4 and 5 and go straight to step 6.)

4 Ask questions to elicit additional information. For example, *At what age are you allowed to leave school? Are there different types of secondary school?*

5 Give a summary at the end and ask your student to correct you.

6 Now ask your student to describe their experience of their education system. How was it similar to or different from the general system? For example, *Although most people in my country start school at six, I started earlier/later because . . .*

7 Finally, contrast the advantages of each system and compare them, or discuss the benefits and drawbacks of the system in your student's country.

8 For homework, ask your student to describe the education system and their experience of it.

Variations

1 For business English, ask your student to describe the health or pension provisions in their company or country compared with the UK or the United States.

2 You could also ask them to describe the vacation allocation system in their company compared with the average company in the UK or the United States.

Box 10.1a: Your education

Age on 1st Sept	SCHOOLS		
3	Pre-School / Nursery School		
4			
5	Infant School		First School
6		Primary School	
7	Junior School		
8			
9			
10			Middle School
11	Secondary School GCSE (General Certificate of Secondary Education) GNVQ (General National Vocational Qualification)		
12		Secondary School with Sixth Form	
13			
14			Upper School or High School
15			
16	Sixth Form A level (Advanced level)		
17			
18+	University or College of Higher / Further Education BA/BSc (Bachelor of Arts/Science) 3–4 years MA/MSc (Master of Arts/Science) 1 year		
	University PhD (Doctor of Philosophy) 3+ years		

Education system in England

From *Learning One-to-One* © Cambridge University Press 2010   PHOTOCOPIABLE

Box 10.1b: Your education

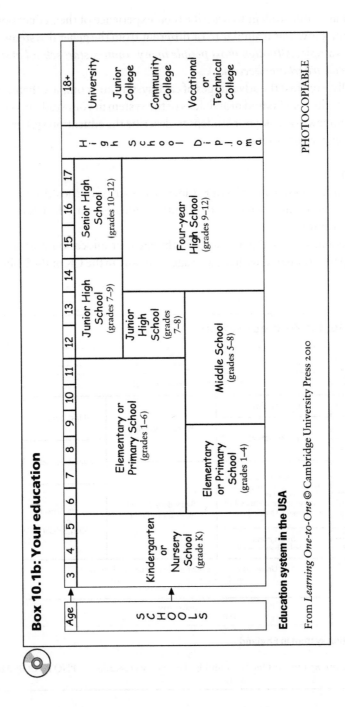

Education system in the USA

From *Learning One-to-One* © Cambridge University Press 2010

PHOTOCOPIABLE

10.2 Career paths

Outline	Your student describes the career structure / job hierarchy in their company and the responsibilities in their job.
Focus	Vocabulary for describing jobs and job responsibilities
Level	Intermediate and above
Time	30–40 minutes
Preparation	None

Procedure

1 Introduce the topic of the lesson: talking about the career structure in the field of your student's occupation/career.

2 Ask your student to describe the hierarchy of job titles in their company and you will try to draw a diagram of it. This will offer your student the opportunity to explain detailed aspects of their company career structure, and for you to ask clarification questions eliciting more description. The diagram may be in the shape of a tree with downward branches, a pyramid or an arrangement of linked balloons. (See *Boxes 10.2a* to *10.2c* on p. 184.)

3 For each job title, try to identify one or two job responsibilities and duties. If your student cannot find a translation, write the word in their native language for later research.

4 To make the diagram more personal, add real names of people in those jobs. You might also talk about the different pay structures of various employees (e.g. Who is paid hourly/monthly? Who gets a bonus?) or their working conditions (Who gets an office? A window? A cubicle? Who works the longest hours?).

5 You may round off this stage by asking your student where on the tree they would like to be in five years' time and what they hope to be doing.

6 For homework, your student can redraw/type the diagram more neatly (perhaps using a different graphic format), filling in any translations as needed and adding more information about each job.

7 In your next class, use the diagram to create scenarios for job-related conversations, problems, dilemmas, e.g. asking for help with a problem, asking for a raise, etc.

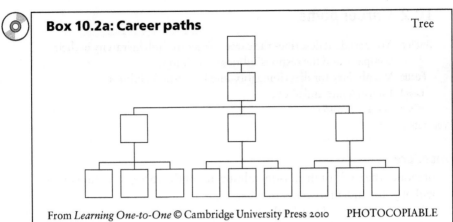

Box 10.2a: Career paths   Tree

From *Learning One-to-One* © Cambridge University Press 2010   PHOTOCOPIABLE

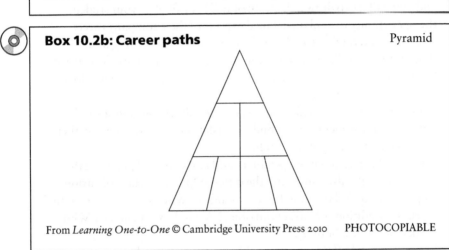

Box 10.2b: Career paths   Pyramid

From *Learning One-to-One* © Cambridge University Press 2010   PHOTOCOPIABLE

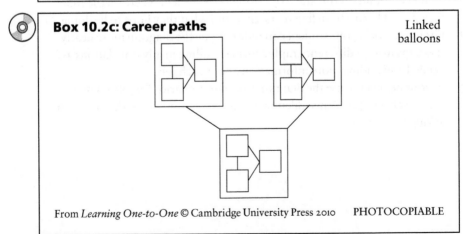

Box 10.2c: Career paths   Linked
                                                                     balloons

From *Learning One-to-One* © Cambridge University Press 2010   PHOTOCOPIABLE

10.3 Steps in a process

Outline	Your student describes steps in a process related to their field of specialization.
Focus	Describing steps in a process, sequence words: *first, then, after that, finally*
Level	Intermediate and above
Time	20–30 minutes
Preparation	Select an audio or a video describing steps in a process related to your student's field (e.g. from YouTube™). Listen to the segment and pick out key words or phrases that can be ordered sequentially. Write them on separate pieces of paper. For example, steps in the judicial process may include the following: being charged, being sentenced, setting bail, going before a judge, being arrested, getting a lawyer.

Procedure

1 Explain the topic you have chosen and ask your student to tell you what they already know about the steps in the process. Possible topics include: steps in a legal/judicial process, steps in the sales process, steps in buying a home, steps in the software development process, steps in starting your own business, steps in developing and testing a new medicine for the market.

2 Ask your student to order the words in the most logical sequence. Use a dictionary if needed.

3 Listen to the audio or watch the video, checking the order as you listen.

4 Ask your student to try to summarize the process to you by describing each step using connector words, such as *first, then, after that, finally*. (You may want to sidetrack slightly to focus on grammar work here, e.g. use of passives, if required.)

5 Listen again to take notes of any other useful words.

6 Repeat step 4, but this time interrupt and ask questions as prompts to help your student expand their description.

7 Finally, role play a conversation between someone asking for advice about the process. Your student will give you advice. (*Tip:* Making some deliberate errors will give your student the chance to correct you politely.)

8 For homework ask your student to prepare a presentation about a process in their job or field.

10.4 Give a guided tour

Outline	Your student describes rooms and buildings in their workplace.
Focus	Describing places, furniture, equipment; modals of obligation, permission and necessity; prepositions of location; passive voice; giving directions
Level	Low intermediate–Advanced
Time	30 minutes
Preparation	None

Procedure

1 Ask your student to draw a plan of their workplace or school.
2 As they draw each room or area, ask questions to help your student describe what each area looks like, is used for and who works there.
3 Your questions can guide your student to use the specific structures you are targeting.
4 If appropriate, your student can draw additional details such as furniture or office equipment on the plan.
5 Finally, role play a visitor to the workplace or school. Your student will play the role of the guide, giving you a formal introduction to each area.

Variations

1 Ask your student to video their workplace or school and talk you through the tour as you watch the video together.
2 Take your lesson outside. Your student might be able to give you a real guided tour of their workplace or school. Other locations that might work for this activity include a zoo, a museum, a library, a supermarket.

Technology option

Ask your student to give you a guided tour of a place they know using Google Maps™ (Streetview) or in a virtual world like Second Life® where they can take you to a city, a building or a site related to their specialist field of knowledge (e.g. architecture, medicine, law).

10.5 Cooking lesson

Outline	Your student teaches you how to prepare a favourite dish.
Focus	Vocabulary for food, measurements, cooking and giving instructions
Level:	Low intermediate–Advanced
Time	30 minutes
Preparation	None

Procedure

1 Ask your student to choose a dish they know how to prepare, perhaps a typical one from their country. Ask them to teach you how to cook the dish.
2 Make a list of ingredients together.
3 Find out which of them are in your (or your student's) kitchen and which of them needs to be bought.
4 Buy the missing ingredients.
5 Cook (and eat) the dish together.

Variations

1 Watch a video on YouTube™ about making a dish that you both like. Use the video as a dictation to make a list of ingredients and instructions. Then make the dish together.
2 Prepare a script for a YouTube video on making a dish. Then make the video.
3 Adapt this to another type of (non-cooking) activity such as instructions for making origami, or playing a board game.

10.6 Business etiquette

Outline	Your student tells you about business etiquette in their (or another) culture.
Focus	Vocabulary for describing polite and impolite behaviour
Level	Low intermediate–Advanced
Time	30 minutes
Preparation	It may help you to do some research on this topic of your chosen country before the lesson (there are some helpful videos on the topic of 'business etiquette differences' on YouTube™).

Procedure

1 Identify a country where your student travels for business, or nationalities of people with whom they often have business dealings.

2 Brainstorm a list of differences between business etiquette in that culture and the student's own culture. Give your learner the opportunity to teach you what they know. Your list may include:

- greetings
- use of names and titles
- business cards
- ways of sitting or standing
- body language / gestures
- meals
- socializing
- gifts.

3 Watch your selected YouTube video together and check off how many of the items on your list were mentioned, adding any additional ones.

4 If suitable you might watch the video with sound turned off and try to guess what the differences are.

5 Role play people from these two different cultures. You might contrast a 'good' and a 'bad' example of social interaction.

6 Ask your student to write a summary for homework. This could be in the form of a letter giving advice to a business person travelling to their country for the first time.

10.7 Museum visit

Outline	Your student tells you about a museum or art gallery in their town.
Focus	Language for asking about opening hours, cost of entry, directions, etc.
Level:	Beginner–Intermediate
Time	30 minutes
Preparation	It may help to look up some website links to museums or art galleries before the lesson, and send them to your student (see the *Websites* section, pp. 202–3).

Procedure

1 Think of a museum or art gallery that you would both like to visit.

2 Prepare a list of questions that a visitor might ask before going to the museum, e.g. *Where is the museum located? How can I get there? How much does it cost? What are the opening hours? Is there a café or restaurant?*

3 For homework, your student will visit the museum webpage and try to find the answers to the questions.

4 In the next lesson, you will role play a visitor calling the museum to find out information. Your student will provide the answers.

5 Follow up with a discussion of what is most interesting in the museum and what you would most like to see there and why. You might plan an itinerary for an afternoon visit.

6 You may also want to evaluate the information on the site and say which aspects of the site were most interesting and useful.

Technology option

1 If you are carrying out this lesson online, you can look at the website together and guide your student to the appropriate places to answer the questions, helping them to understand the navigation tools on the site.

2 Some museums have virtual sites where you can tour the museum online. Or you can visit a museum in a virtual world like Second Life® (see *Activity 9.8: Visiting Second Life*).

10.8 Selling a product

Outline	Your student tells you about their company's products.
Focus	Language for asking about opening hours, cost of entry, directions, etc.
Level:	Intermediate–Advanced
Time	20–40 minutes
Preparation	Find a product label with product information in English, either a real example of the product or from the internet.

Procedure

1 Choose (or ask your student to choose) a product they are familiar with, e.g. contact lens solution or a cold medicine. It should be something that has both positive and negative effects. Bring in an example of the product.

2 Work together to make a list of questions that a consumer might need to ask about the product.

3 Help your student read the product information to find the answers to the questions.

4 Role play a conversation between a consumer and a salesperson about the product.

5 Write a list of key words and expressions that you used during the role play.

6 Make a list of the positive and negative effects of the product.

7 Transfer the language used in this role play to a different product that your student knows well (possibly a product made by their own company).

8 Ask questions to clarify and elicit further description or explanation of what the product does and why it is good.

9 Record the conversation and analyse it for useful expressions and good points as well as errors.

Variations

1 Turn this into a role play where a customer calls up to complain about a product. Your student can then write a letter answering the complaint.

2 Ask your student to find websites where people review the product in order to establish how the product is generally rated.

10.9 Cultural expert

Outline	Your student critiques a text about their culture.
Focus	Language for correcting, clarifying and evaluating
Level:	Intermediate–Advanced
Time	20–40 minutes
Preparation	Find a text/article in English about your student's culture.

Procedure

1 Ask your student to try to read the text from the point of view of a visitor to their country. Ask them to circle the concepts and ideas that are not fully explained in the text.

2 Use small sticky notes of different colours to identify any information that is misleading, any information that is not explained, and places where additional information could be added. (If teaching online, ask your student to highlight the text in different colours.)

3 Discuss with your student the improvements that could be made to the text.

4 Your student then rewrites the text for homework.

Variations

Use a similar text about an English-speaking culture and identify the ideas that are unclear. For homework, your student can do some research to try to clarify them.

If you share your student's culture, use a text about a country that your student knows well but that you do not.

10.10 Writing a description

Outline	Your student tells you about their hobby or free-time activity and uses the information to write an essay.
Focus	Language for describing a hobby
Level:	Intermediate–Advanced
Time	20–30 minutes
Preparation	None

Procedure

1 Explain that you are going to help your student write a description of their hobby and that you are going to start by interviewing them.

2 As they speak, take notes of key words. Write them randomly around a large piece of paper. These words might be adjectives, verbs or nouns that describe specific aspects of the hobby. Try and identify key words that will help your student write a description.

3 Ask questions to get more detailed information and keep adding to the array of words.

4 Ask your student to circle, underline or use coloured markers to categorize the words and to use lines to connect words that go together. You might decide to highlight all feeling-related words, for example, or underline all technical nouns.

5 Ask your student to rewrite the words in categories of their choice. They can also add more words at this stage.

6 Use the categories to develop a topic for each paragraph of an essay. For example:

- Why do you like this hobby?
- What is difficult/interesting/fun about it?
- How did you first become interested in it?
- How can you learn how to do this hobby?
- What type of people like this hobby?
- Where do they do this hobby?
- What facilities or equipment are needed?

7 Decide the best order for a sequence of paragraphs based on these questions.

8 Finally, help your student to write the opening paragraph of their description and ask them to finish it for homework.

Variation
Instead of a hobby, choose another theme related to your student's work, study or other interests.

Technology option
If using an interactive whiteboard, ask your student to move the words around the board to place them in the most appropriate categories.

10.11 Preparing a PowerPoint® presentation

Outline	Your student prepares a PowerPoint presentation.
Focus	Practising presentation skills
Level	Intermediate–Advanced
Time	20–30 minutes
Preparation	None

Procedure

1 Explain that you will help your student to prepare a PowerPoint presentation to help them practise their presentation skills.
2 You may choose to look at some example PowerPoint presentations online or some examples prepared by other students.
3 Help your student choose a topic for a presentation. They may choose to describe themselves, their job or their country, for example. Identify the audience. Choose one of these topics and break it down into sub-topics, each of which could be illustrated by a picture and a bullet list of information points. A possible example could be 'Me and My Job':

   1 Who am I?
   2 What is my job?
   3 What kind of company do I work for?
   4 Why do I like my job?
   5 How is my job changing and why?

4 Work with your student, asking them questions and identifying key points for each slide. Discuss appropriate pictures to go with the key points (your student can find them for homework).
5 In the next lesson, go over useful language for introducing the presentation and for presenting each slide. For example:

   Today I'm going to talk to you about . . .
   I've prepared some pictures to illustrate my presentation.
   First I'd like to tell you about myself . . .

6   Practise useful techniques such as hiding the bulleted list and uncovering it gradually as they go through the information.
7   Ask your student to give their presentation and make an audio recording. Then listen to the recording with your student while watching the slides. Ask your student to note any points that could be improved.
8   Select any of the points that came up for further practice.

Variations

1   If your student needs to make presentations for work, this is an easy introduction to the skills needed. You can apply the same procedure to their real-life topic.
2   Students could also prepare a 'voice-over' and record this on to their PowerPoint presentation, using the narration tool.

Technology option
You could also prepare a more creative and fun presentation with music, photos and voice-over using an online tool such as Animoto® (www.animoto.com) or Kaltura (www.kaltura.com).

Note
Although the end product is important in this activity, the discussion and negotiation that goes on in developing the product will provide intensive speaking, listening and vocabulary work.

10.12 Eating out

Outline	Your student tells you about their favourite type of food.
Focus	Practising vocabulary for food and ordering from a menu
Level:	Low intermediate–Advanced
Time	30 minutes
Preparation	Bring in menus from different restaurants – real, downloaded from the internet or online.

Procedure

1   Find out in advance what kinds of restaurants (e.g. Mexican, Indian) your student likes to go to. Ask them to bring in a menu if possible, or look at some similar menus online.

2   Ask your student to explain all the dishes and how they are cooked. Ask lots of questions about the ingredients, the flavour, etc.
3   Decide which dishes are appealing, healthy, pricey, good value, unusual.
4   Ask them to advise you on the best dishes to choose.
5   Imagine you are in the restaurant and ordering your meal. Your student will play the server.
6   Ask extra questions such as *Does it have any garlic in it? What kind of dressing comes with the salad? Can I have extra tomatoes instead of cheese?*
7   Make your choices and calculate the total cost of your meal.
8   Switch roles and role play again.

Technology option
If you have internet access, look up restaurants online and ask your student to advise you on the best one to go to for a special dinner or party.

10.13 Famous entrepreneurs

Outline	Your student tells you about people they admire.
Focus	Practising vocabulary for describing personal characteristics
Level	Intermediate–Advanced
Time	30 minutes
Preparation	Bring in information about one or two entrepreneurs as a standby. Information about entrepreneurs can be found under 'Business English' in the Websites section, pp. 202–3.

Procedure
1   Ask your student to choose two or three entrepreneurs who are well known in their country.
2   Ask your student to say:

> who they admire most and why
> who they do not admire and why
> who they think is most representative of successful entrepreneurial qualities and why
> who is most unusual in their outlook and why
> what made them successful

3   Use the information gathered from these questions to make a list of qualities that make a successful entrepreneur. Rank them in order of importance.

4 Discuss how these good qualities may also sometimes be bad. For example, someone who is determined may also become stubborn.

5 Try to come up with a definition of the qualities of a successful entrepreneur in your culture compared with other cultures, and discuss how differences in these values may cause misunderstandings.

6 Ask your student to research one successful entrepreneur for homework and tell you about him or her in your next lesson.

Note

This conversation could go in many different directions. It may be very beneficial to understand and make explicit the values of the business culture in your student's context, which are probably quite different from those of an educational context.

10.14 Choosing a home

Outline	Your student tells you the best places to buy or rent a home.
Focus	Practising vocabulary for describing and comparing relative advantages of different types of homes
Level:	Intermediate–Advanced
Time	30–40 minutes
Preparation	Bring in local maps or links to Google Maps™ or MapQuest®, flyers from an estate agent or local newspaper, if available in English, or information from websites advertising properties for sale (there are also many independent sites that collate information from different sources).

Procedure

1 Ask your student to recommend the best districts in which to buy a home. Discuss some of the criteria for choosing a neighbourhood to live in (transportation, schools, shops, etc.).

2 Use a map or go to Google Maps to find the area and look up homes for sale.

3 Discuss your home requirements: How many bedrooms do you need? Would you like a garage, garden, study, etc. Your student can make a list of your requirements.

4 Go to a property sale website and ask your student to recommend two or three homes (or bring in some property-for-sale flyers to the next lesson).

5   Pick the best one and look it up on the map or on Google Maps. Ask your student to give you directions to the places.

6   Role play an estate agent showing the client around the home and trying to sell the home to you.

Variations

Instead of homes, look for the best place to set up a store or a restaurant, or try researching hotels or restaurants and look up sites that have reviews of them (type in the name of the restaurant or hotel + 'reviews').

Thanks to Howard Vickers of Avatar Languages (www.avatarlanguages.com) for suggesting this activity.

10.15 My favourite music

Outline	Your student tells you about their favourite musician or band and/or about music from their country.
Focus	Practising vocabulary for describing music and musicians
Level	Intermediate–Advanced
Time	30–40 minutes
Preparation	None

Procedure

1   Interview your student about their favourite musician or band. Ask them to tell you as much as they can about their background, history, the kind of music they play, why their music is popular, why they like it. Listen to a track or watch a video clip on the internet. Choose a section of a song and transcribe or translate the lyrics.

2   Take notes as you listen, as if you were planning to write an article about this band.

3   Your student can use your notes to create an online presentation about the band (in a blog or a wiki) or create a written presentation for their portfolio.

Variations

Adapt this activity according to your student's interests and interview them about a favourite artist, photographer, architect, dancer, writer or actor.

10.16 Culture exchange board game

Outline	Your student answers quiz questions about the target culture, and you answer questions about the student's culture.
Focus	Comparing cultures, exchanging cultural information
Level	Low intermediate and above
Time	20–30 minutes
Preparation	Bring in a die and two counters (e.g. small buttons or plastic discs). Make a copy of the board game (see *Box 10.16a*) and a copy of one set of questions cut up into squares (see *Box 10.16b*).

Procedure

1 Explain the rules of the board game (1. Roll the die. 2. Pick up a question card. 3. If you answer correctly, move your counter the corresponding number of squares. 4. Go up the ladders and down the snakes. 5. The winner is the person who reaches 'Finish' first).

2 Place the cards face down in the centre of the table. Explain that the questions (*Box 10.16b*) are all about different aspects of your and your student's cultures. The teacher will speak about aspects of the student's culture, the student will speak about aspects of the target culture. This gives your student the opportunity to tell you any information you do not know and to correct you if you are mistaken. (*Note:* This is more of a cooperative activity than a competitive game, so you can give each other hints and clues whenever possible.)

3 While you are playing the game, encourage your student to tell you as much as possible about aspects of their culture by asking additional questions about each topic.

4 As a review, go over the questions and see how much you remember at the end.

Variation

If you share your student's culture, you and your student can both talk about the target culture (one could talk about the USA and the other about the UK, for example). Encourage your student to base their information on personal experience whenever possible so that they are still taking the role of cultural informant.

Box 10.16a: Culture exchange board game

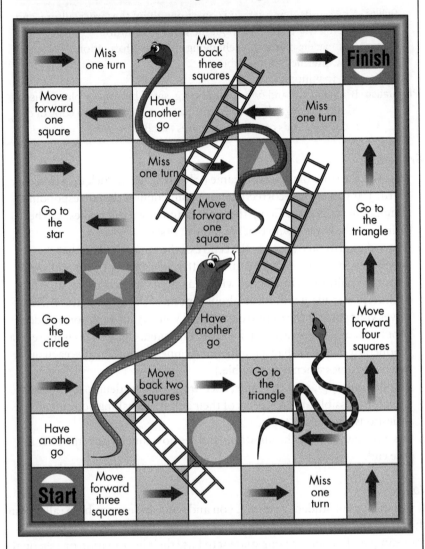

Box 10.16b: Culture exchange board game

Name one festival and three facts about it.	Name one city and three facts about it.	Name one typical food or dish and three facts about it.	Name one famous person and one fact about him or her.	Name one popular film, book, or TV show.
What is one usual greeting?	What is one way of saying goodbye?	What is one non-verbal gesture used to say hello or goodbye?	What do you say before the start of a meal?	What do you say if someone helps you?
What is a typical way to celebrate New Year's Eve or Day?	What is a typical way to celebrate a birthday?	What is a typical way to celebrate a wedding?	What is a typical way to celebrate a new baby?	What is a typical way to celebrate a new home?
What is one popular first (or given) name?	What is one typical family name?	What do people usually eat for breakfast?	What do people usually eat for lunch?	What do people usually eat for dinner?
What is one popular summertime activity?	What is one popular wintertime activity?	What is one popular sport?	What is one traditional product or industry?	What is one historic event?
Name one mountain, river or geographical feature.	What is the size of the population?	Name one traditional type of music or musical instrument.	What colour is the national flag?	Name three facts about the language.

From *Learning One-to-One* © Cambridge University Press 2010   PHOTOCOPIABLE

References and further reading

Course design

Council of Europe (2001) *A Common European Framework of Reference for Languages: Learning, Teaching, Assessment*. Cambridge: Cambridge University Press.

Richards, J. (2001) *Curriculum Development in Language Teaching*. Cambridge: Cambridge University Press.

Swan, M. and Smith, B. (2001) *Learner English: A Teacher's Guide to Interference and Other Problems*. Cambridge: Cambridge University Press.

Feedback

Anderson, K., Benson, C. and Lynch, T. (2001) 'Feedback on Writing: Attitudes and Uptake', *Edinburgh Working Papers in Applied Linguistics* No. 11, pp. 1–20. Available at http://www.eric.ed.gov.

Ferris, D. (2002) *Treatment of Error in Second Language Student Writing*. The University of Michigan Press.

Learner autonomy

Knowles, M. S. (1986) *Using Learning Contracts*. San Francisco, CA: Jossey-Bass Inc., Publishers.

Little, D. (2003) *Learner Autonomy and Second/Foreign Language Learning*. Available at http://www.llas.ac.uk/resources/gpg/1409

Little, D., Ridley, J. and Ushioda, E. (eds.) (2003) *Learner Autonomy in the Foreign Language Classroom: Teacher, Learner, Curriculum and Assessment*. Dublin: Authentik.

Learning styles

Churches R. and Terry R. (2007) *NLP for Teachers: How to Be a Highly Effective Teacher*. Camarthen: Crown House Publishing

Gardner, H. (1984) *Frames of Mind: The Theory of Multiple Intelligences*. London: Fontana Press.

Pritchard A. (2005) *Ways of Learning: Learning Theories and Learning Styles in the Classroom*. London: David Fulton Publishers.

Sprenger, M. (2003) *Differentiation through Learning Styles and Memory.* Thousand Oaks, CA: Corwin Press.

Non-verbal communication

Boyes, C. (2005) *Need to Know?: Body Language.* London: Harper Collins.

Pease, A. and Pease, B. (2006) *The Definitive Book of Body Language: The Secret Meanings Behind People's Gestures.* St Ives: Orion.

Portfolios

Little, D. and Perclová R. (2001) *European Language Portfolio: Guide for Teachers and Teacher Trainers. Strasbourg: Council of Europe.* Also available at http://culture.coe.int/portfolio.

Council of Europe, European Language Portfolio, http://www.coe.int/T/DG4/Portfolio/

British Council BBC website, Teaching English: http://www.teachingenglish.org.uk/think/articles/portfolios-elt

Pronunciation

Baker, A. (2008) *Ship or Sheep? An Intermediate Pronunciation Course.* Cambridge: Cambridge University Press.

Gilbert, J. (2001) *Clear Speech from the Start: Basic Pronunciation and Listening Comprehension in North American English.* Cambridge: Cambridge University Press.

Virtual worlds

Kern, N. (2009) 'Starting a Second Life', *English Teaching Professional,* Issue 61, March, pp. 57–9. See also: Nergiz Kern's blog about teaching in Second Life: http://slexperiments.edublogs.org/.

Vickers, H. (2007) *SurReal Quests: Enriched, Purposeful Language Learning in Second Life.* Available at http://kt.flexiblelearning.net.au/tkt2007/edition-15.

Websites

Here is a selection of websites that I have found useful for dealing with various activities.

Business English
> http://www.bbc.co.uk/worldservice/learningenglish/business/talkingbusiness/
> http://www.better-english.com/exerciselist.html
> http://www.englishclub.com/business-english/
> http://www.entrepreneurs. about.com/od/famousentrepreneurs/
> http://www.financial-inspiration.com/ famous-entrepreneurs.html/

Collaborative activities online
> Make an avatar and record your voice, http:// www.voki.com
> Make a slide presentation with words and music,
> http://www.voicethread.com
> Make a poem by moving words around the screen,
> http://www.magpo.com
> Send a postcard, http://www.postcards.org

Collaborative editing tools
> http://www.docs.googledocs.com
> http://www.etherpad.com
> http://www.twiddla.com

Dictionaries
> http://dictionary.cambridge.org/
> http://www.thefreedictionary.com/
> http://www.freelang.net
> http://www.wordweb.info/free/
> http://www.itools.com

English language learning games
> http://www.manythings.org/
> http://www.a4esl.org/
> http://www.marks-english-school.com/games.html

Grammar resources
http://www.edufind.com/english/ grammar/index.php
http://www.esl.about.com/od/englishgrammar/

Making crosswords and other word puzzles
http://www.puzzlemaker.discoveryeducation.com/
http://www.edhelper.com/puzzles.htm

Museums
http://www.britishmuseum.org
http:/www.moma.org
http://www.metmuseum.org
http://www.vam.ac.uk

Pictures
http://www.flickr.com

Sample résumés and CVs
http://www.bestsampleresume.com/free-resume-samples.html
http://www.cvtips.com/resumes-and-cvs/
http://www.cvcl.co.uk/sampleCVs.htm
http://www.jobsearch.about.com/od/cvsamples/
http://www.eslpages.com/sampleresumeformat.htm

Sample tests and test-taking tips
http://www.examenglish.com/
http://www.studygs.net/tsttak1.htm
http://www.testtakingtips.com/test/
http://esl.about.com/cs/advanced/ht/ht_taketests

Virtual worlds
http://www.secondlife.com
http://www.twinity.com

Webquests
http://webquest.org/index.php
http://www.theconsultants-e.com/webquests/
http://www.nelliemuller.com/ESL_WebQuests.htm

Index

absences 11
accuracy and fluency phases of the lesson 25, 28
active 'learning by doing' lessons 67
active listening 13
activities
  ask me a question 104–5
  ask the right question 123–4
  business etiquette 187–8
  business letters 152–4
  career paths 183–4
  childhood pictures 106–7
  choosing a home 195–6
  choosing a story 174
  choosing categories 132–3
  communication style 155–6
  conversation partner role 101–22
  conversation sampler 143
  cooking lesson 187
  correcting written homework 138–9
  create a multimedia slide show 107
  create a poem online 113
  create an avatar 102
  crosswords and word puzzles 128
  cultural expert 190
  culture exchange board game 197–9
  describe this room 131–2
  designing listening comprehension questions 172
  e-postcards 117
  eating out 193–4
  email follow-up 156–7
  email writing skills 155–6
  environmental issues 113–15
  express your feelings 110–12
  family tree 108–9
  famous entrepreneurs 194–5
  feedback provider role 138–59
  friends and enemies 112–13
  getting to know you 101–2
  grab bag 136–7
  grammar auction 124–5
  guess what I have 115–16
  guessing words from context 175
  guided tour 186
  holiday postcards 116–17
  how green are you? 113–15
  improving your résumé 141–2
  independent learning checklist 160–1
  job interview 144–7
  learner role for the teacher 180–99
  learning from mistakes 158–9
  listen and summarize 173
  listen to the gaps 150–1
  mentor and guide role 160–79
  multimedia slide show 107
  museum visit 188–9
  my favourite music 196
  observer and listener roles 123–37
  phone message 147–8
  phrasal verbs 163–4
  picture dictation 134–5
  power of advertising 118–19
  PowerPoint® presentation 192–3
  problem-solving 179
  pronunciation ranking 167–8
  résumé writing 141–2
  rules and regulations 135–6
  selling a product 189–90
  specialist vocabulary 128
  steps in a process 185
  tell me my story 129
  test-taking tips and strategies 165–7
  timed skim-reading 176
  transcribing a one-minute talk 139–40
  tricky situations 149
  true friends and false friends 164–5
  using your skills 168–9
  verb cards 126–7
  visiting Second Life® 169–71, 186, 188–9
  visiting virtual worlds 169–71, 186, 188–9
  vocabulary ping-pong 162
  webquest 177–8
  well done! 121–2
  what do we have in common? 102–4
  what's the word I need? 126
  wordpool bingo 105–6
  work pie 119–20
  writing a business letter 152–4
  writing a description 191–2
  your earliest memory 130–1
  your education 180–2
  YouTube™ video 187
adapting published ELT materials for one-to-one 72–88
Animoto 193

blogs
ESL and ELT blogs 99
sharing teaching experiences 99
body language 13
cultural taboos 15–16
book report 65–6
breaks in a lesson 15
business English 13, 140, 148, 181
business etiquette 187–8
business letter writing skills 152–4

casual or formal dress 13
closed questions 19
cognates and false friends activity 164–5
collaborative approach
course design 49–50
lesson planning 63–7
lessons 34
Common European Framework of Reference
for Languages (CEFR) 57
communication style 155–6
content, feedback on 30–1
conversation partner role 18–21
teacher talking more than is necessary 20
use of closed questions 19
use of open questions 19
use of scaffolding technique 18–19
waiting for the student's response 19–20
conversation partner role, activities 101–22
ask me a question 104–5
childhood pictures 106–7
express your feelings 110–12
family tree 108–9
friends and enemies 112–13
getting to know you 101–2
guess what I have 115–16
holiday postcards 116–17
how green are you? 113–15
power of advertising 118–19
well done! 121–2
what do we have in common? 102–4
wordpool bingo 105–6
work pie 119–20
cooking lesson 187
Counseling-Learning technique 126
course design 49–59
collaborative approach 49–50
course plan 50–4
evaluative criteria 50
function-based course plan 53, 54
goal setting 53, 55–9
grammar-based course plan 51–2
learning contract 58–9
maintaining motivation 50, 53
means to measure progress 50

objectives 49
personalized feedback on test performance
50
progress reports 50
realistic and achievable goals 50, 53
student input 49–50
testing 50
topic-based course plan 50–1
use of language competence descriptors
57–8
course plan 50–4
cultural differences
absences 11
avoiding misunderstanding 11
body language taboos 15–16
lateness 11
non-verbal communication 13, 15–16
teacher–student relationship 13
cultural expert activity 190
culture exchange board game 197–9

desired outcomes questionnaire 42
distance learning via the internet 1
dress codes 13

eating out activity 193–4
electronic comments and corrections 30–1
email etiquette 11–12, 156
email follow-up 156–7
email tutoring 11–12
feedback from your student 95
feedback to your student 20
making emails friendly and supportive 15
signature function 15
using emoticons 20
ways to encourage your student 20
email writing skills 155–6
environmental issues activity 113–15
errors, approaches to correction 4, 52
error analysis worksheet 52
ESP 140
European Language Portfolio 64
evaluator role 13–14
eye contact 13

family tree activity 108–9
feedback, using text or email 20
feedback from your student 34–5
learner self-evaluation 94–5
reflection on 98
verbal 89–90
written 90–3
feedback provider role 25–31, 99
advantage of one-to-one learning 2, 3
approach to giving feedback 25

feedback provider role (*cont.*)
  balance positive and negative feedback
    26, 29
  electronic comments and corrections
    30–1
  fluency and accuracy phases of the lesson
    25, 28
  language of instruction 30
  meaning and content 30–1
  modelling skills for your student 29
  mutual editing tools 30–1
  opportunities for learning 25
  test performance feedback 50
  types of feedback on speaking 26–8
  types of feedback on written work 29–31
  what kinds of errors to correct 25
  when to correct 25
feedback provider role, activities 138–59
  business letter 152–4
  communication style 155–6
  conversation sampler 143
  correcting written homework 138–9
  email follow-up 156–7
  email writing skills 155–6
  improving your résumé 141–2
  job interview 144–7
  learning from mistakes 158–9
  listen to the gaps 150–1
  phone message 147–8
  transcribing a one-minute talk 139–40
  tricky situations 149
fluency and accuracy phases of the lesson
    25, 28
formal or casual dress 13
function-based course plan 53, 54

Gardner, Howard 24
getting started 6–16
  cultural differences 15–16
  establishing ground rules 11–12
  non-verbal communication 13 15
  setting up a study area 6–9
  signalling phases of a lesson 14–15
  teaching tools 10
goal setting, course design 53, 55–9
Google Docs™ 31
Google Maps™ 186, 195
grammar-based course plan 51–2
grammar practice exercises, adaptation for
    one-to-one 80–3
ground rules for teaching/learning 11–12

holiday postcards activity 116–17
homework, correcting written homework
    138–9

IATEFL 99, 131
independent learning
  checklist 160–1
  developing 32
  strategy development 2, 3
independent study skills, developing 74
internet
  distance learning 1
  VoIP (Voice over Internet Protocol) 15, 143
  see also online tools and resources
internet-based exercise, adaptation for one-
    to-one 84–5

job interview activity 144–7
job/work skills 168–9
job skills and tasks questionnaire 47
journal (student) 32, 38, 95
journal (teacher), reflections on lessons 96–7,
    99

Kaltura 193

language competence descriptors 57–8
language of instruction 30
laptop, uses as a teaching tool 10
lateness 11
learner
  background 37
  language level 37
  see also student
learner autonomy 32
learner-generated materials 71
learner history questionnaire 41
learner log or journal 32, 38, 95
learner role for the teacher
  feedback from your student 34–5
  reflective aspect of teaching 34–5
learner role for the teacher, activities 180–99
  business etiquette 187–8
  career paths 183–4
  choosing a home 195–6
  cooking lesson 187
  cultural expert 190
  culture exchange board game 197–9
  eating out 193–4
  famous entrepreneurs 194–5
  guided tour 186
  museum visit 188–9
  my favourite music 196
  PowerPoint® presentation 192–3
  selling a product 189–90
  steps in a process 185
  writing a description 191–2
  your education 180–2
learner-selected materials 69, 71

learner self-evaluation 94–5
learner takes control 74, 78, 79, 81, 84
'learning by doing' lessons 67
learning contract 58–9
learning materials 68–88
  adapting published ELT materials for one-
    to-one 72–88
  authentic materials 71, 72
  considerations when selecting 68–9
  developing independent study skills 74
  different ways to use the same material 74
  grammar practice exercises (adaptation
    examples) 80–3
  internet-based exercise (adaptation
    example) 84–5
  learner takes control 74, 78, 79, 81, 84
  learner-generated materials 71
  learner-selected materials 69, 71
  listening comprehension exercise
    (adaptation example) 79–80
  modelling tasks for your student 73, 76,
    80, 82, 84, 85, 86, 87
  pair-work activity (adaptation example)
    83–4
  personalization 73, 75, 78, 81, 83, 85, 86,
    87
  planning lessons 73
  reading comprehension exercise
    (adaptation example) 76–8
  recycling the material in different ways 74,
    80, 81, 82, 84, 85, 86, 87
  reflection on choices 69–70
  role play (adaptation example) 87
  role play 74
  role reversal 73, 75, 78, 85
  supplementing published materials 74, 76,
    79, 81
  walk around activity (adaptation example)
    86
  warm-up activity (adaptation example)
    75–6
learning one-to-one
  advantages for students 2, 3
  advantages for teachers 2–3
  challenges for students 3–4, 5
  challenges for teachers 4, 5
  distance learning via the internet 1
  flexibility 1
  nature of the one-to-one relationship 1
  range of content of lessons 1
  teaching context 1
  variety of settings 1
learning strategies, developing 25, 32
learning style questionnaire 43
learning styles 22, 24–5

accuracy or fluency 24
auditory, visual or kinesthetic preference
  24
deductive or inductive 22, 24
preferred intelligences 24
preferred style of learning 24
understanding your own preference 24
using a variety of styles 24–5
lesson
  signalling different phases 14–15, 28
  taking breaks 15
lesson planning 60–7
  active 'learning by doing' lessons 67
  adapting learning materials 73
  aims of each lesson 61–2
  collaborative lesson planning 63–7
  feedback from your student 61–2
  first lesson 60–1
  lesson plan and backup 62–3
  outline of steps for each lesson 62–3
  reading programme 65–6
  recap at the end of each lesson 61–2
  structure of each lesson 61–2
  student portfolio 64
  tasks and activities for each lesson 62–3
lesson planning questionnaire 48
listener role for teacher *see* observer and
  listener role
listening comprehension exercise, adaptation
  for one-to-one 79–80

Magnetic Poetry® 113
MapQuest® 195
materials *see* learning materials
meaning, feedback on 30–1
mentor and guide role 32–3
  collaborative approach to lessons 34
  developing independent learning 32
  developing learning strategies 32
  distinction between mentor and counsellor
    32–3
  encouraging learner autonomy 32
  limits on areas of advice 32–3
  measuring progress 32
  personal advice 32–3
  reflection by the student 32
  sharing the student's expert knowledge 34
mentor and guide role, activities 160–79
  choosing a story 174
  designing listening comprehension
    questions 172
  guessing words from context 175
  independent learning checklist 160–1
  listen and summarize 173
  phrasal verbs 163–4

mentor and guide role, activities (*cont.*)
  problem-solving 179
  pronunciation ranking 167–8
  test-taking tips and strategies 165–7
  timed skim-reading 176
  true friends and false friends 164–5
  using your skills 168–9
  visiting Second Life® 169–71
  visiting virtual worlds 169–71
  vocabulary ping-pong 162
  webquest 177–8
Microsoft® Word, commenting
  electronically 30–1
modelling skills for your student 29, 73, 76,
  80, 82, 84, 85, 86, 87
motivation, maintaining 50, 53
multiple intelligences framework 24
museum visit 188–9
music activity 196
mutual editing tools 30–1

needs analysis 36–49
  learner's background 37
  learner's language level 37
  methods which can be useful 37–9
  needs analysis questionnaires 37–8,
    39–49
  obtaining documents used for work or
    study 39
  placement test 37
  reasons for carrying out 36
  reflective writing 38
  student journal 38
  types of information required 37
  visiting your student's workplace 38–9
needs analysis questionnaires 37–8, 39–49
  desired outcomes 42
  job skills and tasks 47
  learner history 41
  learning style 43
  lesson planning 48
  practical information 40
  wants and needs 46
  your interests 45
  your job 44
Neuro-Linguistic Programming (NLP) 24, 131
non-verbal communication 13–15
  active listening 13
  body language 13
  cultural differences 13, 15–16
  differentiating teacher's roles 13–14
  encouraging your student to talk 13
  evaluator role 13–14
  eye contact 13

formal or casual dress 13
  nodding and smiling 13
  signalling phases of a lesson 14–15
  teacher–student relationship 13

observer and listener role 21–5
  observing learning styles 22, 24–5
  recording your observations 21–3
  reflecting on your observations 21–3
observer and listener role, activities 123–37
  ask the right question 123–4
  choosing categories 132–3
  describe this room 131–2
  grab bag 136–7
  grammar auction 124–5
  picture dictation 134–5
  rules and regulations 135–6
  specialist vocabulary 128
  tell me my story 129
  verb cards 126–7
  what's the word I need? 126
  your earliest memory 130–1
observer notes 21–3
one-to-one relationship, nature of 1
online tools and resources 10, 32
  Animoto 193
  business letter writing 152
  collaborative editing tool 135
  create an avatar 102
  crosswords and word puzzles128
  e-postcards 117
  Google Maps™ 186, 195
  Kaltura 193
  Magnetic Poetry® 113
  MapQuest® 195
  maps 186, 195
  multimedia slide show 107
  poetry 113
  presentation tools 193
  pronunciation practice 167–8
  résumé tools 142
  sample tests 166
  test-taking tips 166
  Twiddla 135
  virtual worlds 169–71, 186, 188–9
  VoiceThread 107
  VoIP (Voice over Internet Protocol) 15,
    143
  Voki 102
  webquest 177–8
  YouTube™ 187–8
  see also internet
online tutoring
  feedback by email 95

using email features 15
webcam 'classroom' 15
open questions 19

pair-work activity, adaptation for one-to-one
83–4
payments 11
personal advice 32–3
Personal Construct Theory 133
personalization of learning materials 73, 75,
78, 81, 83, 85, 86, 87
phone message activity 147–8
phrasal verbs activity 163–4
placement test 37
portfolio 64
PowerPoint®, preparing a presentation
192–3
practical information questionnaire 40
presentations 192–3
professional development 69, 98–9
progress measurement 50
progress reports 50
pronunciation practice activity 167–8

questionnaires *see* needs analysis
questionnaires

reading comprehension exercise, adaptation
for one-to-one 76–8
reading log 65
reading programme 65–6
recycling strategies activity 113–15
reflection (student) 32
reflection (teacher)
choice of learning materials 69–70
on negative student feedback 90
on your observations 21–3
recording your reflections on lessons
96–100
teacher in a learner role 34–5
résumé writing skills 141–2
role play 74
adaptation for one-to-one 87
role reversal 73, 75, 78, 85

scaffolded feedback
speaking 26–7
written work 29
scaffolding technique for helping students
18–19
Second Life® (virtual world) 169–71, 186,
188–9
self-directed learning 53, 58
Skype™ 143

speaking
scaffolded feedback 26–7
types of feedback 26–8
student
advantages of learning one-to-one 2, 3
challenges of learning one-to-one 3–4, 5
encouraging your student to talk 13
history of learning 22
journal or learner log 32, 38, 95
learning style 22, 24–5
stresses on 19–20
see also learner
study area
arrangement of chairs and table 8–9
environmental factors 6–7
setting up 6–9

teacher
advantages of learning one-to-one 2–3
challenges of learning one-to-one 4, 5
development of teaching skills 98–9
teacher roles 17–35
conversation partner 18–21, 101–22
differentiating 13–14
feedback provider 25–31, 138–59
learner 34–5, 180–99
mentor and guide 32–3, 160–79
observer and listener 21–5, 123–37
teacher–student relationship 13
teaching tools 10
TESOL 99
test-taking tips and strategies 165–7
text
feedback 20
ways to encourage your student 20
topic-based course plan 50–1
Twiddla 31, 135

verb cards activity 126–7
video conferencing tools 15
virtual worlds 169–71, 186, 188–9
vocabulary cards 32
vocabulary notebook 32
VoiceThread 107
VoIP (Voice over Internet Protocol) 15, 143
Voki 102

walk around activity, adaptation for one-to-
one 86
wants and needs questionnaire 46
warm-up activity, adaptation for one-to-one
75–6
webcam 'classroom' 15
webquest activity 177–8

work
  describing work activities 119–20
  specialist vocabulary activity 128
written teaching/learning agreement 11
written work
  scaffolded feedback 29
  types of feedback 29–31

your interests questionnaire 45
your job questionnaire 44
YouTube™ 187–8

Zone of Proximal Development (ZPD) 18